THE IVP NEW TESTAMENT COMMENTARY SERIES

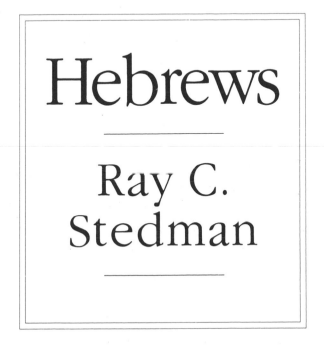

Hebrews

Ray C. Stedman

Grant R. Osborne
series editor

D. Stuart Briscoe
Haddon Robinson
consulting editors

INTERVARSITY PRESS
DOWNERS GROVE, ILLINOIS, USA
LEICESTER, ENGLAND

InterVarsity Press
P.O. Box 1400, Downers Grove, Illinois 60515, U.S.A.
38 De Montfort Street, Leicester LE1 7GP, England

InterVarsity Press, U.S.A., is the book-publishing division of InterVarsity Christian Fellowship, a
... ... ~vement active on campus at hundreds of universities, colleges and schools of nursing in the United States of America, and a member movement of the International Fellowship of Evangelical Students. For information about local and regional activities, write Public Relations Dept., InterVarsity Christian Fellowship, 6400 Schroeder Rd., P.O. Box 7895, Madison, WI 53707-7895.

Inter-Varsity Press, England, is the book-publishing division of the Universities and Colleges Christian Fellowship (formerly the Inter-Varsity Fellowship), a student movement linking Christian Unions in universities and colleges throughout the United Kingdom and the Republic of Ireland, and a member movement of the International Fellowship of Evangelical Students. For information about local and national activities in Great Britain write to UCCF, 38 De Montfort Street, Leicester LE1 7GP.

USA ISBN 0-8308-1815-4
UK ISBN 0-85111-672-8

Printed in the United States of America ∞

Library of Congress Cataloging-in-Publication Data

Stedman, Ray C.
   Hebrews/Ray C. Stedman.
     p.   cm.—(The IVP New Testament commentary series)
   ISBN 0-8308-1815-4
   1. Bible. N.T. Hebrews—Commentaries. I. Bible. N.T.
   Hebrews. English. New International. 1991. II. Title.
   III. Series.
   BS2775.3.S74   1991
   227'.8707—dc20   91-30977
                                    CIP

British Library Cataloguing in Publication Data

A catalogue record for this book is available from the British Library.

| 17 | 16 | 15 | 14 | 13 | 12 | 11 | 10 | 9 | 8 | 7 | 6 | 5 | 4 |
| 06 | 05 |

To Robert W. Smith,
prince of elders and Bible teacher extraordinaire

General Preface

In an age of proliferating commentary series, one might easily ask why add yet another to the seeming glut. The simplest answer is that no other series has yet achieved what we had in mind—a series to and from the church, that seeks to move from the text to its contemporary relevance and application.

No other series offers the unique combination of solid, biblical exposition and helpful explanatory notes in the same user-friendly format. No other series has tapped the unique blend of scholars and pastors who share both a passion for faithful exegesis and a deep concern for the church. Based on the New International Version of the Bible, one of the most widely used modern translations, The IVP New Testament Commentary Series builds on the NIV's reputation for clarity and accuracy. Individual commentators indicate clearly whenever they depart from the standard translation as required by their understanding of the original Greek text.

The series contributors represent a wide range of theological traditions, united by a common commitment to the authority of Scripture for

Christian faith and practice. Their efforts here are directed toward applying the unchanging message of the New Testament to the ever-changing world in which we live.

Readers will find in each volume, not only traditional discussions of authorship and backgrounds, but useful summaries of principal themes and approaches to contemporary application. To bridge the gap between commentaries that stress the flow of an author's argument but skip over exegetical nettles and those that simply jump from one difficulty to another, we have developed our unique format that expounds the text in uninterrupted form on the upper portion of each page while dealing with other issues underneath in verse-keyed notes. To avoid clutter we have also adopted a social studies note system that keys references to the bibliography.

We offer the series in hope that pastors, students, Bible teachers and small group leaders of all sorts will find it a valuable aid—one that stretches the mind and moves the heart to ever-growing faithfulness and obedience to our Lord Jesus Christ.

Introduction

Dr. E. M. Blaiklock, a longtime professor of classics at the University of New Zealand and a noted biblical historian, made the startling statement: "Of all the centuries, the twentieth is most like the first." If that is true, it is evident that twentieth-century Christians should thoroughly understand first-century Christianity. All the New Testament books help us in this regard, but perhaps none so practically as Acts and Hebrews. Preeminently in these two books appear flesh-and-blood believers struggling to overcome the stranglehold of past traditions and adjust to the fresh movements of God in their fast-changing world. Readers of Hebrews in the twentieth century (and the twenty-first) will identify quickly with the first recipients of this letter when they see how they struggled to hold on to their faith in Jesus in the midst of growing world chaos and powerful cultural pressures to return to a more comfortable past.

It seems to me that issues usually handled in an introduction, such as authorship, place of origin, identity and locality of the readers, canonical acceptance, and so forth are best dealt with after, rather than before, the epistle has been studied. Let the letter speak for itself first, and then deal with the questions which reading the letter naturally raise. Presumably, interest in such matters is much higher then, and judgment on the weight of arguments is more precise. Hence my preference would be to put this introduction at the close of the commentary. But some readers may be helped by background information before the letter is read. In deference, then, to long-standing custom this introduction will seek to deal now with the questions of authorship, reader identity and so forth.

It was a standing joke at the seminary I attended for students to ask one another: "Who wrote the epistle of Paul to the Hebrews?" It was admittedly weak humor—on a par with "Who is buried in Grant's Tomb?" But it served to raise a primary question about Hebrews: who actually wrote this brilliant treatise on the person and work of Christ that has been a part of our New Testament from the beginning?

Even the ancient church was uncertain about the authorship of Hebrews. It is not an anonymous letter, since its original recipients clearly knew the writer, but nowhere does he divulge his name. Tertullian (d. 225) reported that current tradition held that Barnabas was the author. Clement of Alexandria (d. 215) thought Paul had written it in Hebrew and Luke had translated it, though the Greek of Hebrews seems too elegant to be a translation. Clement's successor, Origen (d. 254), wrote, "Men of old time have handed it down as Paul's, but who wrote the Epistle God only knows certainly." As we shall see in the commentary the internal evidence of Hebrews argues strongly against Paul's authorship (2:3), but the theology and thinking of Paul are everywhere in the letter. This suggests some close associate of Paul who reflects Paul's theology but brings his own gifts of eloquence and thorough knowledge of Judaism to the writing of this letter.

Four candidates for authorship come to mind: Barnabas, Silas, Luke and Apollos. The first three traveled with Paul extensively and were godly men, well known to many throughout the early church. But neither Barnabas nor Silas appears in the New Testament as capable of writing such a treatise as Hebrews. Barnabas wavered theologically at Antioch under the pressure of Judaists (Gal 2:13) and is seen in Acts as a warm, loving encourager of many, but not as a spokesman or teacher (Acts 14:12). Little is known of Silas, but such silence does not argue well for him being the author of such an outstanding epistle, and the suggestion that he is the author of the letter has gained little support. Luke also has been proposed by Calvin and Delitzsch, and though he surely knew Paul's thinking well, he too does not appear in Scripture as a doctrinal teacher or pastor but rather as a historian. The possibility that he was a Gentile would not explain the intimate knowledge of Judaism which the writer of Hebrews possessed.

That leaves Apollos as the most likely author. He knew Paul well, having taught with him at Corinth. Luke, in Acts 18:24, calls him "mighty in the Scriptures," and his reputation in the church was that of an eloquent orator, well able to marshal arguments in an orderly fashion, just as the writer of Hebrews does. Further, he was a Jew from Alexandria, where the Septuagint originated and was widely employed, and where the religious philosopher Philo had lived and taught. As we shall see, Hebrews quotes the Septuagint without exception, and several scholars have seen the influence of Philo's thought upon some of the ideas presented in the letter (see Spicq 1952). Luther felt that Apollos wrote Hebrews, as do more modern scholars such as Manson, Spicq, Alford, Moulton, Farrar and A. T. Robertson. One argument against Apollos is that the Alexandrian church never credits him with authorship. Even though philosophical and exegetical evidence points to an Alexandrian author, doubt still lingers about Apollos being the one. The question remains open for debate and will probably never be settled till the writer himself in glory makes it certain.

The identity of the recipients of this letter is also difficult to determine precisely. The title "To the Hebrews" was not a part of the Greek text, and certain modern commentators (James Moffat, E. F. Scott, Gerhardus Vos) have even concluded that the letter is addressed to Gentiles. But the constant comparison between Judaism and Christianity found in the letter strongly argues against this. There is also no reference to pagan practices or philosophies which were widespread in the Roman world.

But if the readers were Jewish Christians, where and when did they live? Some expositors favor Palestine and even Jerusalem, but the internal evidence does not support this. The writer admits in 12:4 that they had not yet resisted to the point of shedding blood. This could not be said of Christians in Jerusalem or Palestine, as Acts makes clear. Their obvious interest in and respect for the office of high priest and for the temple, though patently to be expected of Palestinians of Jewish background, would also be characteristic of Jews in the diaspora. The enormous number of pilgrims to Jerusalem during high holy days made this abundantly evident.

The links with Paul's letter to the Colossians, which we will note at several points in our commentary, indicate the readers may be a colony of Jewish Christians in the Lycus valley of provincial Asia. Their geographical nearness to Ephesus would support extensive contact with Apollos and Timothy and help explain the references in Hebrews to Sabbath observance, new moon festivals, food restrictions and especially the worship of angels, which are also treated in Colossians.

Arguments that the readers of Hebrews lived in Rome are based on extensive quotations of the letter by Clement of Rome and the reference of the writer to "those from Italy" in 13:24. As we shall see, the latter reference is so ambiguously put that it can refer to any group of Italian Christians found living anywhere in the empire. Priscilla and Aquila could be a case in point for they are seen in Rome, in Corinth and in Ephesus within the New Testament records. Incidentally, the use of a *masculine* participle referring to the author, in 11:32, rules out Priscilla as a possible author of the letter as a few scholars have proposed. The quotations from Clement merely show that a copy of Hebrews reached him soon after it was written, but the slowness of the churches of the West to accept the epistle as genuine would argue against a Roman origin.

Wherever the readers lived it is clear that they were largely second-generation Christians; their first leaders had already passed away (13:7). They had professed Christ for some time (5:12) and had once shown great evidences of sturdy faith (10:32-34). But when the letter was written they had reached a state of discouragement and spiritual lethargy. Some had given up meeting with other believers (10:25); many found

---

Note: [1]David Gooding in "An Unshakeable Kingdom" captures well the line of rabbinic persuasion that former Jews would have faced when their Christian faith began to waver:

To think that you—you who as Jews have heard the oneness of God proclaimed ten thousand times in your home, in the synagogue, in the temple, ever since you were children—to think that you could be taken in by this fanatical sect who worship the man Jesus as if he were God!

And who are you to say that our high priest and Sanhedrin were wrong to have Jesus crucified? . . . Just because you have heard stories of the miracles Jesus is supposed to have

increasing opposition to their faith in Jesus among their Jewish families and friends, while they also faced sharpening hostility from gentile authorities and citizens.

These conditions indicate a date for the letter toward the close of the sixties of the first century, probably in A.D. 67 or 68. The temple was still standing in Jerusalem, and Jewish rituals were performed there as they had been for centuries. But evidence was increasing that Romans and Jews were headed for a bloody clash. The long-expected return of Jesus to set things aright seemed delayed beyond endurance. Faced with these difficulties some were wavering and wondering if perhaps they had made a terrible mistake; perhaps Jesus was not the Son of God as they had been taught but was only a creature, though perhaps the highest of the angels. He certainly was not what the apostles had claimed him to be. Should they continue to follow the uncertain hope of seeing again one who may have been at best an archangel, or at worst, an impostor?[1]

Certainly such doubts might shake true Christians for a while, and the uncertainty raised by these questions would almost surely turn mere professors away from Christ back to their old faith. It must be made apparent to both that there can be no compromise—it is one or the other, Christ or judgment! So, tenderly, lovingly, with great pastoral concern and care, the writer of Hebrews brings his readers face to face with the central issue: Is Jesus the Son of God or is he not? Is he the great Antitype of all Jewish ritual and sacrifice and the high-priestly Mediator of the new covenant whom the prophets had predicted? Or is he only a man? The choice is plainly stated in 10:39: "But we are not of those who shrink back and are destroyed, but of those who believe and are saved."

Despite the uncertainties that still linger around aspects of the epistle, there is little doubt of its early acceptance within the canon of Scripture. Clement of Rome used it in writing to the Corinthians within the first

---

done and have been impressed by his popular religious propaganda, you imagine he must have been more than human. But our high priest and rabbis knew what they were doing. They saw through his deceptions and had the courage to do what the Bible commands to be done with such deceivers—have him executed.

So be sensible. Stop imagining you know better than your rabbis. Show some respect and gratitude to your father and mother for your upbringing. Come back to the faith of your fathers, and don't ruin your lives and break your parents' heart and disgrace your family by abandoning everything you were brought up to believe by running off with this fanatical sect.

century. The rest of the West was slower in receiving it, perhaps due to its use by the Montanists who were in disfavor as a heretical group. It was not till late in the fourth century that Western churches gave it full acceptance. The Eastern churches had viewed it early as Pauline and received it readily. Polycarp and Justin Martyr both allude to it in their writings, and Irenaeus and Hippolytus seem acquainted with it, though they denied Paul's authorship. In Reformation times, Luther had some misgivings about its content but Calvin regarded it highly, saying, "There is, indeed, no book in Holy Scripture which speaks so clearly of the priesthood of Christ, which so highly exalts the virtue and dignity of that only true sacrifice which He offered by His death, which so abundantly deals with the use of ceremonies as well as their abrogation, and, in a word, so fully explains that Christ is the end of the Law" (Bruce 1964:xlvii).

There are certain striking emphases in Hebrews which mark its uniqueness in the canon of Scripture. No other New Testament book deals as fully as Hebrews with the present priesthood of Jesus. No other book traces both the comparisons and contrasts of that Melchizedek priesthood with the ancient Aaronic or Levitical priesthood. None other urges believers with such passion and confidence to call upon their great high priest for help in daily pressures and trials.

No other letter focuses as fully on the present greatness of Christ as Hebrews, except for the book of Revelation. Passages in Paul, notably in Ephesians and Colossians, briefly extol his exaltation "far above all rule and authority, power and dominion, and every title that can be given, not only in the present age but also in the one to come" (Eph 1:21), but only in Hebrews is this developed to contrast with the great human leaders of the past (Abraham, Moses, Aaron, Joshua) as well as angelic authorities, leaving Jesus as alone occupying the place of ultimate authority in the universe. He shares the very throne of God by right and conquest.

There is also a unique eschatological orientation to Hebrews. Except for Revelation, no other book describes a city of God coming to earth and answering the petition of the Lord's Prayer, "thy kingdom come, thy will be done on earth as it is in heaven." Abraham was the first to see its approach, and Hebrews traces that hope through the centuries by listing the lives of many heroes and heroines of faith (Heb 11), ending with the time of his readers (including us) who "are looking for the city that is to come" (Heb 13:14). That coming city is linked here with "the age to come" which is not put under the authority of angels but of men who share with the Son of Man dominion over all the earth (Heb 2:5-10). In their redeemed spirits believers already live in that city (Heb 12:22-24), but they await its physical appearance upon the earth, as promised to Abraham long before.

Without this epistle in our Bibles today, the people of God would be greatly impoverished. Modern readers may lack the Jewish background which the original recipients possessed, yet the letter forces all Christians of any age to face certain issues: Do we believe that Jesus is God the Son, infinitely higher than any angel, who is both the creator of all things and the final arbiter of all human events? Are we trusting in his death on the cross and his subsequent bodily resurrection as the full and complete ground of our salvation, or are we still looking to some act by us or some ritual or sacrament performed for us to bring us safely to heaven? Do we habitually turn to Jesus as our great high priest, to find inner strengthening to face pressures, resist temptations, conquer guilt, or achieve self-control in daily situations? Are we permitting our cultural context to lure us into practices or deeds that are inconsistent with the new life we have been given in Christ? Do we count it a high privilege to take up our cross daily and glory in bearing his reproach in the midst of a confused and immoral world? Is the expectation of the return of Jesus as King over the whole earth a bright and shining reality to us, frequently renewing our vision and outlook? Do we recognize the loving hand of God upon us in the midst of hardships, disappointments and trials, as strengthening us and also giving us opportunity to display his character to those who are near us?

These are the concerns of the writer of Hebrews. These are the "things that accompany salvation" to which he refers in Hebrews 6:9. They must all become our daily concern if we are to lay full hold of the "better things" which Jesus' birth in Bethlehem's manger introduced. The central thrust of this great letter is summed up in the words of an old hymn:

Rise up, O Church of God
Have done with lesser things;
Give heart and mind and soul and strength
To serve the King of kings.

Outline of Hebrews

COMMENTARY

☐ Greater Than the Prophets (1:1-3)

The epistle to the Hebrews begins as dramatically as a rocket shot to the moon. In one paragraph, the writer breathtakingly transports his readers from the familiar ground of Old Testament prophetic writings, through the incarnation of the Son (who is at once creator, heir and sustainer of all things and the fullest possible manifestation of deity), past the purifying sacrifice of the cross to the exaltation of Jesus on the ultimate seat of power in the universe. It is a paragraph daring in its claims and clearly designed to arrest the reader's attention and compel a further hearing.

These introductory verses present a sharp departure from the usual first-century epistolary practice, as seen so regularly in Paul's epistles. There are no opening greetings, no indication of the writer's name and no expression of good wishes. For this reason some have viewed Hebrews as a formal address, perhaps even a sermon. This idea finds some support in 13:22, "my word of exhortation." But the treatise clearly ends like a letter, with the writer asking his readers to pray for him as he looks forward to seeing them. He also gives them news of Timothy and brings greetings from others.

The Author's Purpose The author intends to present a series of arguments for the superiority of Jesus over all rival claims to allegiance which his readers were feeling and hearing. Their attention was easily diverted off in other directions, just as our attention is easily distracted today. They, like us, were being tempted, frightened or pressured into following other voices and serving other masters. In chapters 1—7, he examines these rival authorities and reveals their inadequacies. None was, in itself, a false or fraudulent voice. Each was ordained by God and proper in its intended place. Each had served the people of God well in the past, and no teaching or expectation was wrong at the time it was given. But now the final word, the ultimate revelation from God toward which all the other voices had pointed, had come. To this supreme voice the author directs his readers' attention, and ours, by contrasting this final word with the past utterances.

First, there were the prophets, God's ancient spokesmen (1:1-3); then the angels, Israel's guardians (1:4—2:18); then Israel's great leader, Moses (3:1—4:7); Israel's godly general, Joshua (4:8-13); and finally the founder of Israel's priesthood, Aaron (4:14—7:28). Each was a voice from Israel's past that needed to be heard but that was woefully inadequate if followed alone. It was clearly a case of the good being the enemy of the best. Eclipsing all these, as the rising sun eclipses the light of the stars, is the figure of Jesus, God's Son, creator and heir of all things. The abrupt beginning here marks the intensity with which the author writes. It parallels, in that respect, Paul's letter to the Galatians. The writer sees clearly that any slippage in the view of Jesus as supreme is fraught with the gravest danger and must be dealt with forthrightly and thoroughly. Since the same danger is present today, Christians must take special care that no obscuring mists of doubt or unbelief should diminish the stature of Jesus in their eyes.

The Primacy of Jesus Jesus' superiority to the prophets is marked in six ways. First, he is the Son, and as such speaks with greater authority and completeness than the prophets. Through them God spoke *at many times and in various ways,* but not always when men desired, nor as clearly as they might have wished. The word spoken through the prophets and that spoken by the Son is marked by three particulars: a

Notes: **1:1** See Westcott for a thorough treatment of verse one, discussing the meaning

contrast of method (various ways), of time (various times), and of agency (in Son), all marking the prophetic revelation as inferior to that which comes through the Son. "What is communicated in parts, sections, fragments, must of necessity be imperfect; and so also a representation which is made in many modes cannot be other than provisional" (Westcott 1889:3-4). F. F. Bruce puts the matter well: "Priest and prophet, sage and singer were in their several ways His spokesmen; yet all the successive acts and varying modes of revelation in the ages before Christ came did not add up to the fullness of what God wanted to say" (1964:3).

God's word through the Son is final and complete. The apostles are but additional spokesmen for Christ, for in their letters they only expand his subject matter and do not add any new teachings or insights. Jesus affirms this superior status himself when he says to his disciples, "Blessed are your eyes because they see, and your ears because they hear. For I tell you the truth, many prophets and righteous men longed to see what you see but did not see it, and to hear what you hear but did not hear it" (Mt 13:16-17).

The phrase *these last days* means more than merely the present time. It looks on to the second appearing of Jesus (9:28) which brings the last days of the present age to an end, to be followed by the new age of the kingdom referred to in 6:5. The appearance of the Son on earth to reveal truth "kept secret from the foundation of the world," also marks the beginning of the last days which continue until he comes again.

Second, the Son's superior greatness to the prophets springs from his position as both creator and heir of all things. Here Paul's argument in Colossians 1:15-17 is perhaps reflected. Creation's beginning and end form the boundaries of time. Jesus stands both at the end of the future and at the beginning of the past. He made this claim himself to the astonishment of the Jews, "Before Abraham was born, I am!" (Jn 8:58). Jesus is also the heir of all creation. The prophets were God's spokesmen, living out their allotted span of time, circumscribed by the events of earth—but Jesus is the eternal Son, who creates, and therefore owns, all things. Westcott sees the absence of the article before *Son* as signif-

---

of *polymerōs* ("at many times") and *polytropōs* ("in many ways") and especially the contrast of the Old Revelation with the New.

icant *(by his Son* is simply "in Son" in the Greek text). He expresses that significance by saying, "[it] fixes attention upon the nature and not upon the personality of the Mediator of the new revelation. God spake to us in one who has this character that He is Son" (1889:7). Though Jesus is clearly superior to the prophets, he does not replace their revelation. The Old Testament remains as valid Scripture for the followers of Jesus, as the author will bring out many times. The prophets were used by God as spokesmen, but the Son, by contrast, "stands" (appointed) as *heir of all things.* Those *all things* refer to the material universe and all forces within it, created by the Son in partnership with the Father and the Spirit.

In the phrase translated *through whom he made the universe* F. F. Bruce sees a trace of a primitive Christian hymn or creedal confession of faith. One finds parallels in similar phrases in John 1:3 and Colossians 1:16. The expressions *the radiance of God's glory* and *the exact representation of his being* also find a parallel in "the image of the invisible God" in Colossians 1:15 and "being in very nature God" in Philippians 2:6. There is no question but that important Christian doctrines were formulated in hymnic style and used widely in early church worship services. Indeed, when a modern congregation sings "Fairest Lord Jesus," they are responding to the same urge that moved the early Christians to praise their Lord.

Third, the Son shares fully in the divine nature. Though our author will argue later that Jesus is also fully man, as other men are, here he unmistakably asserts his deity. *The Son is the radiance of God's glory.* Radiance is light that streams forth from a source of light. As no one can separate the sun's light from the sun itself, so also no one can separate the nature of Christ from that of his Father. Whether the radiance is seen as reflected brightness or inherent brightness, the thought is clear: in Jesus we see

---

1:2 The vastness of the created universe has become more mind-boggling as scientists receive information transmitted back to earth by interplanetary machines. New objects discovered in space, such as black holes, quasars, novas and so forth challenge astronomers and physicists to solve ever more complex riddles. Rather than finding answers to old questions, science is finding more and more questions. This in no way threatens Christian faith in Jesus as Lord in his universe. Rather, it enhances his majesty immeasurably and should cause us to bow in marvel and wonder at the thought that such a Being should consent to redeem us at the infinite price of the cross.

1:3 On the relationships among the persons of the Trinity, I would recommend Wood 1978. Eschewing such feeble illustrations of the Trinity as an egg or the three forms of water,

the essence of God. He is, therefore, *the exact representation of his [God's] being.* As a coin reflects the exact image of the die, so the Son reproduces the precise character (Gk *charakter*—used only here) of the Father. Thus Jesus could say to Philip, "Anyone who has seen me has seen the Father" (Jn 14:9). No more powerful expression of the deity of Jesus is possible. Any attempt to place Jesus as simply the highest product of creation will fail because the evidence is decisive for the contrary. Many sects have tried to teach that Jesus is only human, but they have no scriptural basis to do so.

This full statement leads naturally to the fourth aspect of the Son's work as the master of the universe: *sustaining all things by his powerful word.* This statement of Hebrews is a direct challenge to modern scientific humanism as well as to the older Deism. F. W. Grant states, "There is thus no thought in Scripture of a creation which shall be sufficient for itself, a perfect machine made to run eternally without the Hand that made it" (1903:15). As scientists probe the nature of the universe they increasingly confront the mystery of an unweighable, invisible force which literally holds all things together. This force is identified here as the powerful word of "One who carries all things forward on their appointed course" (Bruce 1964:6). The thought includes more than mere sustaining (as an Atlas holds the world on his shoulders), but expresses movement and progress toward an appointed end. It results in what scientists call "laws of predictability," and so technology becomes a source of evidence for a God-ordered world. New objects discovered in space, such as black holes, quasars and novas, present new problems for astronomers and physicists. These new questions ought not to threaten a Christian's faith. Rather, they can enhance it as God's power and majesty is revealed more and more as our knowledge is increased.

Wood shows how the truth of the Trinity is stamped on all the universe in the basic structure of Time, Space and Matter, revealing clearly how the Son manifests the exact character of the Father.

The use of the Greek *charaktēr* ("exact representation") is a strong argument against the claim of groups like Jehovah's Witnesses who present Jesus as the highest of God's creation, but not himself sharing the nature of God. To support this claim the Jehovah's Witnesses publish their own edition of the Scriptures which mistranslates Greek texts such as John 1:1 and Colossians 1:15-17 to support their position. The claim that Jesus represents in human form the exact character of God is astonishing but too well supported by the Scriptures to deny.

Fifth, in sharp contrast to this image of universal power is the sentence: *After he had provided purification for sins.* This evokes all the agony and blood of the cross. In doing so, the Savior accomplishes something which no prophet or sage of the past nor philosopher or scientist of the present could ever do. Mere power, even vast, creative power, cannot help here. "The glory of God is not the glory of shattering power, but the glory of suffering love" (Barclay 1957:5).

Certain manuscripts emphasize the uniqueness of this act by adding the words *by himself.* This stresses the preciousness of redemption. It was not something done through an impersonal provision; it involved the very heart and soul of the Redeemer and the shedding of his life's blood! Even if the phrase is omitted the thought is retained by the middle form of the verb. The terrible problem which human sin presents can be solved by one, and only one, remedy—the death of Jesus. This is the central theme of the epistle, to which the writer returns many times. It forms the ultimate and final word to man, uttered by the Son and far more significant than anything which has gone before or could ever follow. Creation rests upon power, but redemption upon the sacrifice of one who was "crucified in weakness." He rose and now is seated at the right hand of our majestic God in heaven.

Sixth, Jesus sat down to give expression to his cry from the cross, "It is finished!" The phrase *sat down at the right hand* is meant symbolically, not literally, for God has no right hand. It denotes the supreme honor accorded to the triumphant Lord, who is risen from the dead. Surely it is a reference (the first of five in Hebrews) to Psalm 110, "The LORD says to my Lord: 'Sit at my right hand until I make your enemies a footstool for your feet.' " Of this Bruce says, "Ps. 110 is the key text of this epistle" (1964:8). That Jesus saw himself in the psalm is evident by his words to the Sanhedrin, "From now on, the Son of Man will be seated at the right hand of the mighty God" (Lk 22:69). In Hebrews 10:11, our author will contrast the seated Messiah with the Aaronic priests who must stand as they offer sacrifices, because Jesus ended the need for further sacrifice forever. That act of redemption reaches out to include the material creation as well as man (Rom 8:20), so that finally nothing remains untouched by its transforming grace. Paul argues this eloquently in Colossians 1:19-20 and Ephesians 1:9-10.

Clearly the world we live in today is one which desperately needs redemption. In this introductory paragraph Jesus has been portrayed as the supreme Prophet, the unique Owner of all things, the uncreated Creator, the exact Image of God's being, the Sustainer of the universe, the Sacrificing Priest who cleanses sin, and the Conqueror who occupies the place of honor above all his creation. From this lofty beginning the writer will assert the supremacy of Jesus above all other names of honor in Hebrew thought or practice. He turns now, in 1:4—2:18, to consider the sharp contrast between Jesus and the angels.

□ Greater Than the Angels (1:4—2:18)

The nation was startled when Nancy Reagan was reported to be influencing her husband's decisions on the basis of advice obtained from her astrologer. Perhaps what is even more startling is to realize that pastors preaching to evangelical congregations today may very well be addressing some, if not many, in their audience who are worshiping angels. There may well be a woman in the fifth row who consulted her horoscope before coming to church. Some teenagers may be involved with experiments with Ouija boards or "channeling" to obtain guidance in important decisions. Perhaps someone has already accepted the teaching of reincarnation as the explanation of what happens to humans after death. As many know, the New Age movement of the late twentieth century encourages such teachings, calling fallen angels *avatars* or *spirit-guides.* Their human devotees practice channeling or mediumistic activities, offering to awaken hidden powers within men and women which will help them fulfill their greatest possibilities. Every pastor must ask, What does the writer of Hebrews say that will help those who, knowingly or not, are drawn to such teaching?

Obviously the teaching is not new. It has been present in every century since the earliest times. The writer sees his readers as under attack from such ideas and understands that he must deal with this first because these attacks threatened their view of Jesus and his pre-eminence. Even angels could challenge this truth. But why would angels pose a threat? Surely the Jewish background of these readers would suffice to prevent them from honoring angels above the Savior. The words of the First Commandment are clear: "Thou shalt have no other gods before me!" It is evident from

Paul's letter to the Colossians that those with a strong Jewish background (Col 2:16-17) could also "delight in false humility and the worship of angels" (2:18). The danger then is apparent: "Those to whom this letter is sent were entertaining, or being encouraged to entertain, teaching which elevated angels, or particular angels, to a position which rivalled that of Christ himself" (Hughes 1987:51-52). If we think this was only a first-century phenomenon, we should remember the way humans have always responded to manifestations of supernatural beings by treating them as gods, or at least demigods, and giving obeisance to them. Indeed, the apostle John twice falls at the feet of the angel who was his guide and is rebuked for so doing (Rev 19:10; 22:8-9).

But their difficulty only serves to underscore the nature of their error. They were being pressured by their former Jewish leaders and also by pagan contacts to view Jesus not as God but as merely a man, and therefore less than the angels. Angels had played a powerful role in Israel's past. There is no record in the Old Testament of an angelic messenger whose message was rejected or whose person was attacked or stoned. When an angel spoke, people listened (Henrichsen 1979:24). The writer acknowledges this impressive impact in his warning of 2:2.

This exaltation of angels above Jesus is intolerable to the writer of Hebrews. He devotes a major passage to its answer, supporting the infinite superiority of Jesus over angels with several reasons. They are his superior name of Son (1:4-5); the command to angels to worship him (1:6); the nature of angels versus the nature of the Son (1:7-14); the great danger of ignoring the Son (2:1-4); his glory as risen and enthroned man (2:5-9); his work as the author of human salvation (2:10-13); and his unique ability to help the recipients of grace (2:14-18). With these seven points, the writer reveals Jesus as the worthy object of praise and worship which not even the most glorious angel could claim.

His Superior Name of Son (1:4-5) The passage from 1:5 to 1:14 constitutes a marvelous choreography of Old Testament passages which,

Notes: 1:4-5 Hughes (1987:52-53) ties this passage with the expectations of the Qumran community rather than with Paul's warning in Colossians 2:18. But in either case Jesus was being subordinated to an angel or angels, and this constituted the danger which is faced in Hebrews.

like a well-programmed ballet, catches immediate interest with a pas-de-deux of two Messianic phrases: one from Psalm 2:7 and the other from 2 Samuel 7:14. Both center on the name of *Son* which must belong properly to Jesus and to no one else. These verses distinguish him from the Father, but also place the Father's imprimatur on his brow.

It is true that angels are called "sons of God" in the book of Job (1:6; 2:1; 38:7 KJV) because, like Adam, they are direct creations from God's hand. This fact may seem to mark angels as equal with Jesus and therefore proper objects of worship. But Jesus is God's Son from all eternity—the uncreated Son. Furthermore, the quotation from Psalm 2 highlights Jesus' status as the exalted Son of Man, as Paul declared in his sermon at Pisidian Antioch (Acts 13:33) referring to his resurrection from the dead. Thus he was both the eternal Son and the glorified human Son (Son of God and Son of Man).

The writer here especially claims the superiority of Jesus over the angels as the Son of Man. No angel could claim either eternity or resurrection as the basis of his sonship, but Jesus had both. Though the angels collectively were called sons of God, no individual angel ever is given that title, or singled out as having a unique status before God. So the writer demands rhetorically, *To which of the angels did God ever say, "You are my Son; today I have become your Father"?*

Psalm 2 is specifically applied to Jesus in Revelation 12:5 and 19:15 and to those who share his kingdom reign in Revelation 2:27, especially in conjunction with the words "you will rule them with an iron scepter" (Ps 2:9). Several scholars have felt that Psalm 2 represents a coronation liturgy which was included in enthronement ceremonies of the Davidic dynasty. One of the rabbis in Midrash *Tehillim* says of Psalm 2:7, "And when the hour comes, the Holy One—blessed be He!—says to them, I must create him a new creation, as it is said, 'This day have I begotten thee.' " Of this F. F. Bruce says, "The implication here seems to be that Psalm 2:7 refers to the time when Messiah, after suffering and death, is brought back to the realm of the living" (1964:13, fn. 63). This under-

---

1:5 The angel Gabriel told Mary at the annunciation that the child to be born would be called "the Son of the Most High" (Lk 1:32). Also at Jesus' baptism the Father's voice proclaimed, "You are my Son whom I love" (Mk 1:11), and again at the transfiguration, "This is my Son" (Lk 9:35).

standing would agree with Paul's use of Psalm 2:7 in Acts 13:33 and clearly the word *today* refers to the resurrection of Jesus rather than the day of his birth in Bethlehem, or of his baptism in the Jordan.

The second source of support from the Old Testament draws on 2 Samuel 7:14. Historically the words "I will be his father, and he will be my Son" were spoken to David concerning Solomon when the prophet Nathan told David that Solomon will build a house for God in Jerusalem. There is, however, a hint that David's power would extend to his progeny, which would also include the Messiah. The prophets in later times spoke often of a greater son of David who would fulfill all the promises to David of an eternal reign. Bruce quotes from the Dead Sea Scrolls where 2 Samuel 7:14 is linked with an expectation of the imminent restoration of David's house by the "shoot of David," the Messiah (1964:14). Note again how the human nature of the Lord is underscored by his title Son of David. As the risen Man, he claims the throne of David, but as such the Father calls him "my Son." By these two quotations, with their royal implications, the writer of Hebrews claims that being related to God as a Son is a far greater title than any angel could claim. This rests on the base of a shared eternity and a resurrection, which is the "new creation."

The Angels Commanded to Worship (1:6) The angels were created, but the Son is begotten. His superiority is now upheld by a verse from the Septuagint version of Deuteronomy 32 which commands all angels to worship the Son (v. 43 LXX). The passage is the Song of Moses uttered before the crossing of the Jordan. At that time Moses said to the people:

1:6 Kistemaker (1984:40) has a helpful note for those who might be troubled by the failure to find any reference to the worship of angels in the Hebrew text of Deuteronomy 32:43 or in English versions based on that text. He says:

The writer of Hebrews quotes from the Hymn of Moses as it was rendered in the Septuagint. The Greek translation of Deuteronomy 32 was well known to him and his audience because in the dispersion the Jews used the Septuagint in the synagogues. The early Christians adopted the liturgy with variations to express the Christian emphasis.

The author's use of a quote from the Septuagint that is without an exact equivalent in the Hebrew text in our possession does not mean that the doctrine of inspiration has been undermined. The Holy Spirit, who is the primary author of Scripture and inspired every human writer, directed the author of Hebrews to select a quote from the Hymn of Moses in the Greek. When the author incorporated the line into his epistle, that line

"Take to heart all the words I have solemnly declared to you this day. . . . They are not just idle words for you—they are your life" (Deut 32:46-47). Allusions to this hymn are found in eleven books of the New Testament (twice in Hebrews—1:6 and 10:30), which indicates its importance to early Christians. In the Song of Moses, the angels are called to worship Yahweh (Jehovah). New Testament writers apply such passages without hesitation to Jesus. Many places in Scripture witness the obedience of the angels, notably Job 38:7, Luke 2:13, and Revelation 5:11-12. Mark 3:11 indicates that even the demons (fallen angels) fell down before Jesus when they saw him and addressed him as the Son of God.

Since the earliest times, Christian commentators have differed on what the *again* refers to in verse 6. If it is taken with the verb *he says* ("he says again"), as in the NIV, it simply means another quotation that supports the superiority of Jesus. If, however, it is linked with the verb *brings* ("he brings again"), it is a reference either to the coming of Jesus at the Incarnation, his reappearance after the resurrection, or his Second Coming at the end of the age. In view of the connected character of these quotations, it seems best to take it as a second support citation, "he says again." Twice in Hebrews, Jesus is called *firstborn* (here and in 12:23). In this verse it seems to refer to his creative work. Bruce rightly says, "He is called 'the firstborn' because He exists before all creation, and because all creation is His heritage" (1964:15). Paul's great assertion is recorded in Colossians 1:15, "the firstborn over all creation." The point of it all is: He whom the Hebrews thought to be subordinate to angels is the very one whom the angels are commanded to worship as their creator!

became inspired Scripture.
For a thorough study of the meaning of *prototokos* ("firstborn") in Hebrews, see Helyer 1976. Jehovah's Witnesses in their New World Translation claim that the title "firstborn of all creation" means that Jesus is the first created being, based on the analogy of a human family where the first-born child is younger than his parents. To support this they must insert the word *other* into Col 1:16: "For by him all *other* things were created." But there is no support for this in the Greek text. They also ignore the fact that in the Old Testament there are several instances where the son designated the firstborn was not the one born first. Ishmael was thirteen years older than Isaac, but it is Isaac who is the firstborn. Though Esau was born first, Jacob becomes the firstborn. Even with Joseph's sons, Mannaseh and Ephraim, a transference of the right of firstborn is made by Jacob when he prays for the two, making Ephraim, the younger, the firstborn.

The Nature of Angels vs. the Nature of the Son (1:7-14) In 1:7-14 the author for the third time sweeps through the Psalms to display a chorus of verses that praise the Son who has a nature inherently superior to angels. In the Hebrew of Psalm 104:4 the natural elements of wind and fire are called the messengers of God; in the Septuagint it is the angels who are made to be these elements. Though they are as powerful as the wind and can be as destructive as lightning, they are, nevertheless, only messengers of the Son while Jesus is the Son of God himself.

This sharp contrast is sustained also by two verses coming from Psalm 45:6-7. Their antiphonal character with verse 6 is clear in the way they are introduced: *In speaking of the angels he says, . . . But about the Son he says . . .* Psalm 45 is a wedding song, originally describing a king of Israel, but later understood by the rabbis as messianic. The contrast between a royal personage and his servant-companions is the point of the quotation. This king is addressed twice as God; possesses a throne, a scepter and a kingdom; loves righteousness and hates wickedness; has a special anointing of joy; and continues as king forever and ever. No angel could claim these attributes. The cause of the king's joy is traced to his love of righteousness and hatred of wickedness. Here, by contrast, may be a hint of the moral defection of the host of angels who fell with Satan. Angels could and did sin, but the Son's love of righteousness kept him safe through the most severe temptations. Even those unfallen angels who also, presumably, love righteousness do so on the basis of choice, while the Son's love of righteousness is inherent in his very nature. For this reason *(therefore)* God has set him above his companions.

Once more our author displays the dazzling glory of the Creator, who is infinitely superior to any angel, by summoning the words of Psalm 102:25-27: *In the beginning, O Lord, you laid the foundations of the earth, and the heavens are the work of your hands.* This is not simply a restatement of truth he has already declared ("through whom he made the universe"—v. 2), but the point he now twice asserts is the timeless endurance of the Son: *They will perish, but you remain; . . . they will be*

1:9 Bruce, Morris, Kistemaker and others see the "companions" of the King as the Christians described in Heb 3:14 and called his "brothers" in 2:11. Hughes does not agree with this. Since Jesus is often seen in Scripture as accompanied by great hosts of angels (Mt 25:31;

changed. But you remain [Gk "you are"] the same. He will make the point again in 13:8, "Jesus Christ is the same yesterday and today and forever." Psalm 102 is addressed to Yahweh by a sorely afflicted suppliant who feels the brevity of his own life in light of the heavens and the earth. But even they shall pass away in due course, like garments that grow old and are changed. This is a marvelous poetic description of what scientists call the law of entropy, or the second law of thermodynamics, which views the universe as running down. But the Creator is above his own laws and remains unchanged forever. These words, applied unhesitatingly to Jesus, place him as far beyond the angels.

As a finale for his presentation of Old Testament support for the superiority of the nature of the Son over that of angels, the author returns to his mildly scornful rhetorical question: *To which of the angels did God ever say, "Sit at my right hand until I make your enemies a footstool for your feet"?* This second reference to Psalm 110 restates the thought of 1:2, "whom he appointed heir of all things." Even his enemies will find their place at the Son's feet when God's purposes are fulfilled. It reflects Paul's declaration in Colossians 2:15, "And having disarmed the powers and authorities, he made a public spectacle of them, triumphing over them by the cross." The cross won the beginning of the ultimate triumph, but its fulfillment awaits the return of Jesus as King.

Contrasted to this Supreme Conqueror, the writer asks, *Are not all angels ministering spirits sent to serve those who will inherit salvation?* Even the mightiest angel is under orders to the Son of God, and gladly helps in fulfilling his desire to bring many sons to glory (2:10). Though the author does not enlarge on the specifics of angelic ministry here, it only requires a review of Bible stories to see that such ministry involves protection (Ps 91:11), guidance (Gen 19:17), encouragement (Judg 6:12), deliverance (Acts 12:7), supply (Ps 105:40), enlightenment (Mt 2:19-20) and empowerment (Lk 22:43), as well as occasional rebuke (Num 22:32) and discipline (Acts 12:23). Their service is rendered largely unseen and often unrecognized, but a passage like this should make us watchful for such help and grateful to the gracious Lord who sends angels to our aid.

2 Thess 1:7; Jude 14) and since the context of Hebrews 1:4-14 is clearly a contrast between the Lord and angels, it seems most probable that angels are the companions referred to in the psalm.

The Great Danger in Ignoring the Son (2:1-4) Having proved beyond all argument that angels cannot compare in importance, power or glory to the Son of God, our author now raises a warning voice against taking lightly what the Son has said. This is the first of five major warning passages in Hebrews, each designed to prevent a specific form of unbelief. The five warnings are found in 2:1-4, 3:12-19, 6:4-8, 10:26-31 and 12:25-29. Our author is deeply concerned lest his readers succumb to the pressures they were feeling and either renounce the gospel outright or gradually turn from public confession and lose its influence entirely. The danger faced in this first warning is that of drifting away from truth. A dramatic word is employed for "drift away," *pararreō,* which means "to flow by" or "slip away from." It describes that carelessness of mind which, perhaps occupied by other things, is not aware it is losing ground. Plato used it of something slipping away from the memory, and Plutarch of a ring slipping from a finger. Another figure often suggested is that of a ship loose from its moorings. The danger highlighted is that of a great loss *occurring unnoticed.* The cause is not taking seriously the words spoken to them. Inattention or apathy will rob them of their treasure.

With these words, the writer reveals his shepherd's heart, since he is not content with instructing the mind with intriguing doctrine. He also longs to reach the heart and move the will to action. The remedy urged is *pay more careful attention* to the things heard (from the Son). This would suggest the frequent reading or hearing of the four Gospels, which contain the actual words of Jesus, and a repeated and careful reading of the further exposition in the Epistles. To neglect or ignore these is to be in deadly danger of drifting away from essential truth, and losing, by default, the *great salvation* which the Son has brought. It is not necessary to openly renounce the gospel. One can remain lost by simply and quietly drifting away from hearing it, or hearing it with no comprehension of the seriousness of its message.

2:1-3 It is a great mistake to set the law and the gospel in opposition to one another. Westcott is right when he remarks: "Throughout the Epistle the law is regarded as a gracious manifestation of the divine will, and not as a code of stern discipline" (1889:37). Similarly, Bruce observes, "In this epistle, moreover, the law is not a principle set in opposition to

The word *salvation* forms the link between chapters one and two. The chapter division was not intended by the writer, who moved immediately *(dia touto,* "therefore") to draw a practical conclusion to the truth he has presented. *Sōtēria,* "salvation," is found seven times in Hebrews, more than in any other New Testament book. In Zechariah's song concerning his son John the Baptist (Lk 1:67-79), he says that the Baptist's ministry was "to give his people the knowledge of salvation through the forgiveness of their sins" (Lk 1:77). Salvation, then, begins with a moral cleansing and in later New Testament development includes justification, sanctification and, finally, glorification with Christ. As Brown astutely observes, "The author is deeply persuaded that a personal relationship with Christ expressed in repentance and faith determines the believer's salvation. But in the teaching of the letter salvation is clearly portrayed as an ongoing process" (1982:24). That Jesus, "the author of their salvation" should have achieved it only by being made "perfect through suffering" (2:10), makes salvation an infinitely precious gift in the eyes of this author.

And that anyone should prefer the ministry of angels, who mediated the giving of the law, to the salvation available in the Son was almost incredible to him! "Come on," he seems to say, "haven't you heard what I've been saying? You value highly the law, though it was given only by angels, but you pass lightly over the final word from God which came in the flesh and blood, and through the death and resurrection, of the very Son of God himself." Both Paul (Gal 3:19) and Stephen (Acts 7:53) acknowledge the part angels played in the giving of the law, though the Old Testament is almost silent about it. Deuteronomy 33:2 and Psalm 68:17 represent only vague references to angels present at Sinai.

But to ignore even the law's partial revelation carried with it certain inevitable consequences *(just punishment*—2:2). Even under the law the divine principle which Paul affirms ("God cannot be mocked; a man reaps what he sows") was operating. The Old Testament gives countless

---

the grace manifested in Christ's saving work, but rather an anticipatory sketch of that saving work" (1964:28-29).

2:3 If the writer had himself heard Jesus he would have undoubtedly said so. Instead he speaks gratefully of the confirming ministry of those who did hear him. It is noteworthy that he does not quote the word of Jesus anywhere in this epistle.

illustrations of this truth. Yet, "if the breakers of the law did not go unpunished, certainly despisers of the gospel cannot expect to do so" (Hughes 1977:73). To ignore the *great salvation* found in Jesus is to find oneself unable to escape the consequent wrath of God, and the judgment of hell. There is no other offer of release!

How great this salvation was is seen in three measures. First, its proclamation began with Jesus himself! This great fact astonished the writer of Hebrews from the beginning of his letter. The incarnate Son has himself announced the impact of his redemptive work upon the cross, and even before that work was accomplished. Mark 1:15 records Jesus as saying, "The time has come. The kingdom of God is near. Repent and believe the good news!" "From the moment of his public appearance to the day of his ascension, Jesus unfolded the full redemptive revelation of God" (Kistemaker 1984:59). So much greater was this announcement than the help which the law held forth that Jesus could say to his disciples: "I tell you the truth, many prophets and righteous men longed to see what you see but did not see it, and to hear what you hear but did not hear it" (Mt 13:17).

Second, though verse 3 suggests that the writer of Hebrews did not personally hear the good news from the lips of Jesus, he says, it *was confirmed to us by those who heard him.* These were surely the twelve apostles and perhaps others as well. This statement rests the gospel securely on eyewitnesses who recorded accurately what they both saw and heard (1 Jn 1:3; 2 Pet 1:16). But, as Hughes observes, this apostolic witness "goes back, not just to the apostles, but through the apostles to the Lord" (1977:79). It was he who sent them forth and promised them the Holy Spirit to bring to their remembrance whatever he had said to them (Jn 14:26).

This implication of the writer that he had not personally heard the Lord removes the twelve apostles as possible authors of this letter—and also virtually rules out Paul (as Luther, Calvin and others have pointed out) since Paul stoutly asserts in Galatians 1:1 and 1 Corinthians 15:3 that he had not obtained his gospel from men but directly from the Lord. He must be included as one of those who had heard the Lord, and the writer of Hebrews does not claim this for himself.

But it is not simply on human memories that the authenticity of the apostolic gospel rests, as the writer adduces a third confirmation of great importance. *God also testified to it by signs, wonders and various miracles, and gifts of the Holy Spirit distributed according to his will.* Just as the Father had borne witness to the Son by signs and miracles (Jn 5:36-37), so he worked with (Gk *synepimartyrountos,* "testifying with") the apostles and others, confirming their word by similar signs and wonders and gifts of the Holy Spirit. The authority from which the gospel flows include all three persons of the Godhead: Father, Son and Holy Spirit. The Son makes the full announcement of it and completes the basis for it through pain and blood; the Father works with him to confirm his word with signs and wonders; and the Spirit continues the confirmation by distribution of spiritual gifts.

John, in his Gospel, tells us that the miracles were "signs," symbols whose meaning revealed the nature of God. John, Matthew and Mark also call them "wonders," that awaken awe and fear; the Synoptists frequently refer to "miracles," or more properly "powers." All three terms appear often in Acts, especially the first fifteen chapters, and mark the validation by the Father to the ministry of the early preachers of the gospel.

The phrase *gifts of the Holy Spirit distributed according to his will* is a bit ambiguous. Taken objectively, it means "gifts which the Holy Spirit distributes." Subjectively, it refers to the imparting of the Holy Spirit himself, as distributed by God. Paul, in his list of spiritual gifts in 1 Corinthians 12:7-11, says, "All these are the work of one and the same Spirit, and he gives them to each one, just as he determines." The last phrase would slant the decision on Hebrews 2:4 toward the objective meaning, that spiritual gifts are given to each believer by the Spirit as the continuing witness of the Spirit to the truth of the gospel.

Do the *signs, wonders and various miracles* also continue throughout the present age? It is impossible to set aside the testimony of Christians through the centuries to the miracle-working power of God in human lives. Many well-attested occurrences of such miracles have been recorded throughout the church centuries, including today. Missionaries and Christian workers of the most sterling character have reported such miracles in widely separated places and cultures so that it cannot be said that the age of miracles ever ceased.

But it must also be remembered that both Jesus and Paul warn clearly that as the age draws to its close there will be manifestations of counterfeit miracles, signs and wonders, done through Satanic agencies, which will deceive many (see Mt 24:24 and 2 Thess 2:9)! It is the effect of these signs and wonders on the lives of those involved which will reveal the genuine teachers from the false ("By their fruit you will recognize them"—Mt 7:15-16). It must also be considered that the profound power of the mind upon the body often produces dramatic improvements in health. But these are not always, or even frequently, associated with religious influence. They are scarcely to be equated with the healings recorded in Scripture, which usually consist of the kind Jesus described to John the Baptist's disciples: "The blind receive sight, the lame walk, those who have leprosy are cured, the deaf hear, the dead are raised" (Mt 11:5).

But let us not lose our way at this point. The concern of Hebrews is not to defend miracles but to warn against losing the *so great salvation* by a careless inattention to its content or its practice in daily life. An individual's response to these great truths determines his destiny. Leon Morris well says, "This Epistle leaves us in no doubt but that those who are saved are saved from a sore and genuine peril. Christ's saving work is not a piece of emotional pageantry rescuing men from nothing in particular" (quoted in Brown 1982:52). Neglecting the word of angels brought immediate earthly consequences; ignoring the salvation of the Son, confirmed by decades of divine ministry through godly men and women, results in eternal tragedy beyond description.

Jesus' Glory As Risen and Enthroned Man (2:5-9) Still thinking of the supremacy of the Son over angels, our author, in 2:5-9, approaches the theme from a different view. In chapter 1 the deity of Jesus was primarily in the foreground; in chapter 2 his perfect humanity means that he is the superior of every angelic being. Verse 5 carries forward the subject of verse 4, *It is not to angels that he [God] has subjected the world to come, about which we are speaking.*

2:5-18 This section affords an excellent basis for a sermon or sermons on the work of Christ. In this brief paragraph we learn that Jesus' death and resurrection accomplished at least four great transactions on our behalf:

1. He recaptured our lost destiny (vv. 5-9).

Some fascinating themes are introduced by this observation. It raises immediately the question, What is meant by *the world to come?* It can mean (1) life after death, (2) the future kingdom of Christ on earth (the millennium) or (3) the new heavens and the new earth. Since almost nothing is said in Hebrews about life after death (9:27), (1) can be dismissed without further development for it is obviously not what he refers to in the phrase *about which we are speaking.* That limiting phrase probably looks back to 1:11-12 which emphasizes the changes which the material creation will experience. Paul, in Ephesians 2:7, speaks of "coming ages," indicating that at least two more ages lie ahead. The two which Scripture continually name are the restored Davidic kingdom (the millennium) and the new heavens and the new earth. In several places Scripture describes the new heavens and earth as lasting forever, intimating it would be the last age yet to come. But the word *world* (Gk *oikoumenē*) in 2:5 refers not to the cosmos, but to the inhabited earth, and this would strongly suggest the writer has in mind (2), the kingdom of Christ on earth. Hughes calls the world to come, "the age of the Messiah in which the messianic promises and prophecies of old find their fulfillment" (1977:82). It is surely to this that Jesus refers in Matthew 19:28, "Truly, I say to you, in the new world *[palingenesia,* 'restoration'], when the Son of man shall sit on his glorious throne, you who have followed me will also sit on twelve thrones, judging the twelve tribes of Israel" (RSV). Several passages in Hebrews (6:5 and 12:22-24) suggest that this kingdom is in some sense already available to those who live by faith. Perhaps, we should see this new age to come as spiritually arrived, yet physically still to come.

A reference to the new heavens and new earth seems unlikely in view of the mention of judgment in Matthew 19:28, for sin will have no place in the new creation. Also Israel will not play a distinctive role among the nations, for then "the kingdoms of this world are become the kingdoms of our Lord, and of his Christ; and he shall reign for ever and ever" (Rev 11:15 KJV).

---

2. He recovered our lost unity (vv. 10-13).

3. He released us from Satanic bondage (vv. 14-15).

4. He restores us in times of failure (vv. 16-18).

If, as the writer claims, the world to come has not been subjected to angels, it raises the possibility that the present age is subject to angelic governance. F. F. Bruce supports this view, citing the LXX rendering of Deuteronomy 32:8:

When the Most High gave to the nations their inheritance

When he separated the children of men,

He set the bounds of the peoples

According to the number of the angels of God.

He further quotes Daniel 10:20, which names angelic beings as "the prince of Persia" and "the prince of Greece," and Daniel 10:21 and 12:1 speak of Michael as "the great prince" who champions the people of Israel (1964:33). This concept would explain why the fallen angel called Satan is referred to as "the god of this world" and is permitted his control until the Lord returns and the new age begins and the curse is lifted from nature. Then, too, the devil will be bound and cast into a bottomless pit for a thousand years (Rev 20:2-3).

This background serves to give special meaning to the quotation from Psalm 8 which the writer of Hebrews now invokes. His vague reference to his source (Gk "Someone somewhere has testified") is not due to uncertainty but to a desire to stress Scripture as speaking, not a mere human author (Bruce, Kistemaker and Hughes). David's psalm is a wondering reaction to the majesty of the night sky as it reveals the power and wisdom of God and forces the question, What part do puny human beings play in such a universe? The answer is that we were made a little lower than the angels, but then crowned with glory and honor, and everything has been put under our feet. This is a direct reference to Genesis 1:26:

Then God said, "Let us make man in our image, in our likeness, and let them rule over the fish of the sea and the birds of the air, over the livestock, over all the earth, and over all the creatures that move along the ground."

Here is glory and honor (made in the image and likeness of God) and authority and power (ruling over all the earth). Some commentators take the *made a little lower than the angels* in a temporal sense, "made for a little while," to imply that human existence in this space-time continuum is only for a brief lifetime, and then we are freed to live the life of eternity. Whichever way the phrase is read, it is clear that our intended destiny was one of power and authority over all the conditions and life of earth. If this was our commission from the moment of creation, what light it sheds on our responsibility to care for this planet and its creatures! We were not given dominion so the earth and the animals should serve us; rather, we are given authority to develop them to the fullest extent intended by the fruitful mind of the Creator. We are to serve them by thorough knowledge and loving care, in the form of servant-leadership which the Lord himself manifested when he came.

Yet, says this writer in what must be the understatement of the ages, *we do not see everything subject to him.* No, there are many things fallen humans cannot control: the weather, the seasons, the instincts of animals, the tides, our own passions, international events, natural disasters, and on and on. The increasing pollution of the planet, the spread of famines and wars, the toll taken by drugs, accidents and disease, all tell the story of a lost destiny.

But almost with a shout the author cries, *But we see Jesus!* He is the last hope of a dying race. And that hope lies both in his deity and his humanity. He alone, as a human being, managed to fulfill what was intended for us from the beginning. When we read the Gospels, we are forced to ask, Who is this man who stills the winds and the waves with a single word; who multiplies food at will; who walks on the waves; who summons fish to bring up coins at his command; who dismisses disease with a touch; and calls the dead back to life? Who is he? He is the Last Adam, living and acting as God intended us to act when he made us in the beginning. It was the First Adam who plunged the race into bondage and limitation; it is the Last who sets us free in soul and spirit, so that we may now learn how to live in the ages to come when the resurrection gives us back a body fit for the conditions of that life.

The writer traces in terse phrases the steps Jesus took to solve forever the problem of human sin. (1) He *was made a little lower than the angels.* There is the whole wonder of the Incarnation; in John's phrasing, "the Word became flesh and lived for a while among us." Then (2) *because he suffered death,* he was (3) *crowned with glory and honor* and thus he achieved *as a human being* the position intended for us in the beginning: the being who was to be closest to God, higher than any angel, and in authority over all things! Then, lest we should forget the cost, the writer adds (4) *so that by the grace of God he might taste death for everyone.* To *taste death* does not simply mean to die, but to experience death in its full horror and humiliation. He comes under the penalty of sin in order that he might remove it. The emphasis here is that what Jesus did through his death and exaltation was *for everyone.* Salvation is now open to all; no one who comes to Jesus will ever be refused. His death was for everyone in the sense that everyone was thereby rendered savable.

Ever since the death of Jesus the way to glory has always included a death which leads to life. Some forms of media-evangelism have presented the Christian life as the way to fulfillment of great possibilities without also making clear that it includes a death to self-indulgence and learning obedience. We dare not extol the incredible benefits of the Christian life without reminding ourselves that they will also lead us to a cross.

To whom, then, is *the world to come* subject? Not to angels, that is clear. It is to be subject to the human race—to the human race as God intended us to be, redeemed and restored through sharing the life of the Man in glory, seated at the right hand of God. This is the theme of verses 10-13.

Jesus' Work As Author of Salvation (2:10-13)

Commentators on Hebrews have pointed out that there is no reference to the love of God in this epistle. Though technically this is true, a text such as 2:10 reveals that behind the suffering and sacrifice of Jesus is the heart of a Father who longs to bring *many sons to glory.* Though the Father was in full control of all forces and events in the universe *(for whom and through whom everything exists),* it was necessary that he subject his beloved Son to a degree of agony and humiliation that could alone fit him to carry out that purpose. This is clearly the meaning of *make . . . perfect through suffering.* Jesus had always had a perfect

---

2:12-13 Hughes has a helpful note concerning New Testament use of Old Testament quotations. He says, "A noteworthy aspect of the New Testament is the manner in which it shows that Christ and his apostles, when they cited passages from the Old Testament, did not flourish them in isolation as proof-texts uprooted from their environment (something

character since his birth; perfection of function required the whole process of incarnation, ministry, death and resurrection. But it was love for the lost human race that drove *both* Father and Son to choose that process.

Thus did Jesus become *the author of . . . salvation.* Other versions substitute "pioneer" (RSV), "captain" (KJV) and "leader" (NEB), for "author." The Greek word *archēgos* implies someone who initiates or originates a plan or program for others to follow. Every American knows that in 1804-1806 two explorers, Captain George Clark and Captain Meriwether Lewis, were sent by President Thomas Jefferson to find a way across the old, trackless West from St. Louis to the Pacific Coast. Such an exploration involved tremendous preparation, special provisions and wise decisions. It was accomplished through great danger and many hardships, as the Lewis and Clark journals make clear. When the explorers returned the whole American West lay open to development. This is the thought behind the word *archēgos.* Jesus, our *archēgos,* opened up a completely new spiritual country, the realm of universal dominion for the human race, which was originally intended for us but was lost by Adam. Those who follow Jesus now are fitted and trained to live in that new world as they walk in the footsteps of him who has gone before.

This concept fits well with the thought of verses 11-13. These describe the Savior and his redeemed as belonging to one family who share the same nature. *The one who makes holy [sanctifies]* is Jesus who had, first, to solve the problem of sin before he could apply it to *those who are made holy,* the redeemed. The act of making holy implies the impartation of a new life, the life of God himself since only God is holy. Those who by faith become sons of God are *made holy* (sanctified) because they share the life of the Son of God. John 1:12 declares, "To all who received him, to those who believed in his name, he gave the right to become children of God," and 1 John 5:11-12 adds, "God has given us eternal life, and this life is in his Son; he who has the Son has life."

Because of this shared life the writer of Hebrews can say they are,

Satan is adept at doing, Mt. 4:6) but had careful regard to the context from which they were taken. The full significance of a statement can be appreciated only against the background of its total context" (1977:107).

literally, "all of One" *(ek henos pantes),* which refers to the Father. (The NIV's *of the same family,* to my mind, somewhat weakens the force of this declaration.) Jesus, who is of different rank and origin, still is *not ashamed to call them brothers.* Since he has made them holy by impart-ing his own life to them, he cannot deny the very holiness he has given. Now the groundwork is laid for believers to learn to live everyday on the basis of the new men and women they have become rather than continuing to live on the old level of humanity they had once been. It is Paul's constant exhortation: "Put off the old man; put on the new." The writer of Hebrews urges the same activity in 12:14. Holiness of nature is the possession of all true Christians; holiness of behavior is to be their goal. But even before that goal is attained to any appreciable degree, it is still true that *Jesus is not ashamed to call them brothers.* The picture is that of an oldest son affirming to another his pride in his younger siblings, even though they do not always act in ways pleasing to him.

To support this wonderful fact, the writer summons three texts from the Old Testament. The first, verse 22, from the well-known Messianic hymn, Psalm 22, reflects the praise of the resurrected Lord as he shares with his brothers and sisters the glories of God's grace. He appears as their teacher, opening their eyes continually to the wonders of the Father whose family they have joined. They then join him in sharing those wonders with the whole congregation. The quotation suggests that his reason for not being ashamed of them is because they share with him the endless adventure of discovering the full meaning of the name of God.

The second text, from Isaiah 8:17, expresses the common sense of dependence which children share toward God; and the third, Isaiah 8:18, recognizes the relationship of children as all equally under the care of one father. Isaiah 8, from which these verses are taken, is the prophet's prediction of a great invasion of Assyria into the land of Judea. Yet in the face of that terrible threat the people are exhorted to continue to trust the Lord Almighty and to wait for his deliverance, though it seem de-layed. The Messiah is seen as "a stone that causes men to stumble and a rock that makes them fall," and it is of him that Isaiah cries, "I will put my trust in him. Here am I, and the children the LORD has given me."

It is easy to see how our author saw these verses as a description of Jesus and his faith-siblings (Christians). That first-century world was coming apart at the seams, just as Isaiah's world had been. And just as Isaiah and his children looked to their invisible Lord for help, so Jesus stands ready to support those who take refuge in him from the threats of a crumbling world.

These two texts, in their original setting, were part of a prophecy of an event yet 100 years in the future, and beyond this, reached to the coming of the Messiah both in his first and second comings. To apply fragments of such prophecies to the Hebrews' circumstances may seem strange to us, but this is fully in line with the use of the Old Testament by all the New Testament writers. The specific verses quoted here are all found in a messianic context.

Jesus' Unique Ability to Help (2:14-18) Drawing on his use of Isaiah's quotation, the writer picks up the word *children* and declares, *Since the children have flesh and blood, he too [Jesus] shared in their humanity.* This description of the Incarnation answers fully all docetic notions that his humanity was simply a phantom appearance. The purpose of Christ becoming a flesh-and-blood man was to enable him to die: that is the startling claim of verse 14! In Charles Wesley's great hymn "And Can It Be?" he begins a verse:

'Tis mystery all, the Immortal dies!
Who can explore that strange design?
In vain the first-born seraph tries
To sound the depths of love divine!

How can one who is immortal die? That is a puzzle which even the angels could not solve. But the Son of God solved it by becoming flesh and blood. He took upon himself our humanity which, even in perfection, was doomed to die (as happened to Adam and Eve). Yet this must be balanced by the gospel's statement that Jesus did not have to die (as all of us must), but gave up his life voluntarily. And die he must if he was to deal with the great enemy of all flesh and blood—death! Behind death the writer sees the power of Satan, who uses God's righteous judgment against sin to bring to death all human beings who sin. But when God's Son willingly entered the dread realm of death on behalf of the race, he could not be held there because he himself was sinless. By his resurrection he broke the power of death over all who accept his invitation to share his risen life. He rendered impotent *(katargeō—*"to annul," "to make inoperative") the devil's power to carry out the full effects of death—that is, spiritual separation from God forever. Physical death remains for all, believers and nonbelievers alike, the transition point between this life and the next. But for believers the "sting of death" is gone, the grave no longer has its victory (1 Cor 15:54-57)!

But this is not a blessing to be obtained only in the future. It has an immediate effect as well, delivering the redeemed from all fear of death, and so liberating them from a lifelong bondage. Since death is the absence of life, spiritual death is already present in human affairs, appearing as depression, fear, boredom, despair, waste, limitation and defeat (Rom 8:6—"The mind set on the flesh is death"). The devil's lie is to convince many that they can avoid such experiences by amassing wealth, maintaining youth by strenuous exercise or expensive treatments, searching for adventure, falling in and out of love, gaining the marks of success, indulging in widespread travel, satisfying every whim, and so forth.

It is the fear of that kind of death which creates the frantic restlessness found in so many. That unsatisfied restlessness, that yearning for what cannot seem to be found, is at least partly what the writer here means by *slavery.* Like a slave bound to a cruel master human beings find themselves forced to keep searching for what they never attain. They try everything, but nothing satisfies. There is pleasure and fun—but seldom peace and contentment. Soon everything palls and the search must begin again. It is a *lifelong* bondage, for the quest never ends till life itself does. No better example of this futile search can be found than Howard Hughes. Bill Hybels recounts his quest for more money, more fame, more sensual pleasure, more thrills, more power, and concludes, in the end "he died a billionaire junkie, insane by all reasonable standard."

But even on our deathbed the bondage is not over, for there again

---

2:16 Hughes (1977:115-18) questions the NIV translation *it is not the angels he helps.* The Greek *epilambanō* is frequently translated "to take hold of" or "to appropriate," and the KJV reflects this, translating the phrase "he took not on him the nature of angels." Scholars through the Reformation took the phrase in that sense and not until the seventeenth century

lurks the dread question, What lies beyond?

Against all this stands the words of Jesus, "Whoever finds his life will lose it, and whoever loses his life for my sake will find it" (Mt 10:39). He came to *free those who all their lives were held in slavery by their fear of death.* His method was first to impart a new life to all who come to him, and join them to a great family of similarly reborn brothers and sisters. Then, through his word, he instructs them in how that new life should be lived and promises the Spirit himself who accompanies the believer throughout his entire journey, teaching him how to turn from the world's ways and Satanic wiles to loving relationships and fruitful service until at last he grows old and steps, through death, into glory and power that beggars description. "The man or woman who lives by this principle will find that for them the devil is impotent" (Stedman 1974:30). James writes, "Resist the devil, and he will flee from you" (4:7). Thus freedom from the lifelong bondage of self-serving is clearly included in the victory of Jesus over death!

If it seems that the writer has drifted far from his intent to show the superiority of Jesus over angels, verse 16 brings us back directly to the point: *For surely it is not angels he helps, but Abraham's descendants.* Only by living himself as a human being could he fully sympathize with, and therefore help, those who struggle with great temptation on their way to glory. The term *Abraham's descendants* clearly envisions Paul's declaration, "If you belong to Christ, then you are Abraham's seed, and heirs according to the promise" (Gal 3:29). This help for Abraham's struggling spiritual descendants is not offered to angels (who are neither redeemed nor Abraham's seed), but it is constantly available to those who come to Jesus as their *merciful and faithful high priest.* It is mercy which he shows toward sinners; faithfulness is exhibited before the Father. This is the first designation in Hebrews of Jesus as high priest, and introduces a theme which will become a major emphasis in chapters 7 through 10.

The record of the four Gospels gives us the details of how Jesus was

and later did the thought "it is not to angels that he gives help" become accepted. Both thoughts are consistent with the immediate context. He took upon himself, not the nature of angels, but of humanity in order that he might help, not angels, but the seed of Abraham.

made like his brothers in every way. Everyday he felt the perturbations caused by living in a sinful world; he knew disappointments and sorrows, physical pains and frustrations of spirit; he grew weary and sore and must often have longed for home and comforts; he was lied to, falsely reproved, argued with, disliked and cheated. The earthly temptations which he endured in the wilderness and at other times (Lk 4:13) from the devil, and daily from the "opposition from sinful men" (12:3), including even his own disciples, made him a sympathetic priest. By virtue of his atonement (propitiation) he can make effective intercession before the Father for any who bring their burdens to him. The fact that he *made atonement for the sins of the people* lifts him to an incomparable level of priestly help. No priest under the law could do that, except in a symbolic and token fashion. But Jesus not only holds forth the hope of finding forgiveness of sins, he has actually taken them away already! To be able to be both merciful toward sinners and faithful to a holy God is possible only because the offense of sin before God has been removed.

The genuine humanity of Jesus reminds him continually of the way temptation feels to us when we are under assault, and his atonement overcomes any limitation of help caused by our sins, so that he may uphold us with both sympathy and integrity before the Father. "If anybody does sin, we have one who speaks to the Father in our defense— Jesus Christ, the Righteous One" (1 Jn 2:1). Bruce puts the case well: "A high priest who has actually, and not merely in symbolism, removed His people's sins, and therewith the barrier which their sins erected between themselves and God, is a high priest worth having" (1964:53).

What a Friend we have in Jesus,

All our sins and griefs to bear;

What a privilege to carry,

Everything to God in prayer.

So the section concludes, and the writer completes his arguments. How can anyone, given the facts, continue to follow angelic guidance (be it from demigod, avatar, spirit guide, ancient master) when the Son of God

---

Notes: 3:1 Though it was Moses' brother Aaron who was high priest of Israel by title, it was Moses and not Aaron who interceded for the people before God (Ex 32:11-14).

himself has come, before whom all the angels, fallen or unfallen, are commanded to worship; for whom angels are but messengers committed to do his wishes; who has himself revealed a far greater message than the Law; and who has recaptured for all who come to him the lost heritage of creation; who has lifted, through the ultimate personal sacrifice, the terrible burden of sin and guilt which lies on us all; and who offers to us each day an inner supply of strength and wisdom for the journey through life? What angel can do all or any of that?

☐ Greater Than Moses (3:1-19)

Houses come in many sizes and designs. The first house my wife and I lived in was a tiny building in Hawaii which served as a parsonage for a church where I was not the pastor (they had none at the time). It had only one bedroom, one bath, a tiny kitchen and a small living room. It's long gone now, and over the years we have lived in several houses. Our last one in California had five bedrooms and three baths and was a virtual mansion compared to the first. But all the houses we have lived in have had two things in common: a preconceived design and a builder.

In Hebrews 3, the writer turns from the angels to compare Jesus to Israel's greatest and most revered leader, Moses, whose primary honor was that he *was faithful as a servant in all God's house. But,* he immediately adds, *Christ is faithful as a son over God's house.*

As in many chapter divisions in the New Testament, the opening words could as well have been the closing words of the previous chapter. The *therefore* ties them together and introduces a fifth title for Jesus thus far in Hebrews: Son, Firstborn, Lord, High Priest and now Apostle. We are encouraged to *fix [our] thoughts on Jesus, the apostle and high priest whom we confess.* The recipients of this encouragement are called *holy brothers* and those *who share in the heavenly calling.* These phrases represent a delicate shift from a well-known Jewish-Christian description ("brothers") to that which is distinctively Christian, and not Jewish ("heavenly calling"—Eph 1:3; 2:6). This explains his plea to look beyond Moses and Jewish things to Jesus, who combines, in his divine-

Exodus 4:14-16 indicates that God permitted Aaron to share the ministry which was originally intended only for Moses.

human person, both functions which Moses exercised (apostle and high priest). However, Jesus fulfilled these to a loftier and far greater level.

What Is God's House? (3:1-6) The reference to Moses' faithfulness in God's house looks back to Numbers 12:7-8 where God describes to Aaron and Miriam how he spoke to prophets in visions and dreams. He continues: "But this is not true of my servant Moses; he is faithful in all my house. With him I speak face to face, clearly and not in riddles." Though several commentators take "God's house" to refer to the nation of Israel, it is better to link it to the tabernacle. Its precursor is the Tent of Meeting, where God spoke these words, and the typology of which is developed more expansively in Hebrews 9. The tabernacle is called "the house of God" at least six different times in the Old Testament, and its successor, the temple, is so designated 43 times. Moses is especially connected with the tabernacle as the one who received its design on Mount Sinai and oversaw its building and ritual. If the tabernacle was the symbol of the dwelling place of God in the midst of his people, as will be seen more fully in 3:6, then we may view the phrase *God's house* as referring both to Israel and the building itself, each standing for the other.

At any rate, the meaning of verses 3-5 is clear: the builder of a house is more worthy of honor than the house which he builds. The house is only the product of the builder's skill and wisdom. Overall conception and the design of infinite detail originates in the mind of the architect-builder; the house simply makes it visible. Thus, Jesus, as the agent of God in building all things, is more worthy of honor than Moses, who was just a servant in the house which the Son was building. This is support for the argument of the existence of God. Cornell University astrophysicist Carl Sagan and many others today insist that we are alone in the cosmos; the cosmos is all there is. If every earthly house shows the design and craft of a builder, how much more does the universe reflect, in its complexity and interrelatedness, a Mind and Hand that put it all together? This Mind and Hand belongs to Jesus as John 1:3 and

---

3:6 The KJV adds the words "firm unto the end" which NIV, RSV and NEB regard as an

other Scriptures attest. As the builder of everything, he outranks even a faithful servant like Moses, who served in the house Jesus made.

The phrase *testifying to what would be said in the future* supports the idea that the tabernacle, with its intensive typology, would teach future generations much about human nature, God and redemption. Stephen, in Acts 7:44, says, "Our forefathers had the *tabernacle of the Testimony* with them in the desert. It had been made as God directed Moses, according to the pattern he had seen." This is expanded in chapter 9 where we shall learn much more about this idea of testifying about the future.

But Christ is faithful as a son over God's house, declares verse 6. *And we are his house* introduces a theme which will become dominant throughout the rest of the letter. The role of a servant and of a son in a house are worlds apart. I recall in my high-school days in Montana a visit I made to a large cattle ranch on the Missouri River as a friend of one of the cowboy employees. We slept in the bunkhouse with the rest of the help and had no access to the main quarters. We rode a couple of rather scruffy horses, and I was involved in helping him do certain assigned chores. Later I visited the same ranch as a friend of the son of the ranch's owner. What a difference! We had the run of the big house, ate in the main dining room, rode the best horses on the ranch and could go anywhere at any time. It made me forever aware of the difference between a son and a servant. The author wants to make this difference clear to his readers' minds also.

It will become readily apparent in chapter 9 that the reality which the tabernacle pictures (and which harmonizes the two peoples of God, Israel and the Church), are human beings themselves. The writer declares: "We are his house!" It is redeemed humanity who is to be the dwelling place of God (1 Cor 6:19; Eph 2:22; Rev 21:3). The writer has just presented Jesus (in chapter 2) as the Man who fulfills God's intent for the human race. That ultimate intent is that we may be indwelt by God. This is surely the meaning of Jesus in John 14:20, "On that day you will realize that I am in my Father, and you are in me, and I am in you."

---

insertion from verse 14. The thought of continuance is still there even if the phrase is omitted.

glory that you gave me, that they may be one as we are one: I in them and you in me."

Again, in John 17:22-23, he prays to the Father, "I have given them the

These concepts are revolutionary to the Jewish mind, as Jesus himself understood in trying to teach them to his disciples, and as the writer of Hebrews realizes as he seeks to lift his readers to views of themselves which they had only grasped dimly, if at all. At this point he ventures to use for the first time the Greek term for the Messiah (*Christ*—literally, "anointed") and so help turn their minds from Jewish hopes to the "better things" of which the Jewish shadows spoke.

We [believers] are his [Christ's] house, he asserts, *if we hold on to our courage and the hope of which we boast.* This *if* has troubled many people for it seems to imply that being a member of Christ's house can be lost after it is gained by wavering in our courage or hope. But the statement is more likely *descriptive* rather than *conditional.* It tells us that courage *(parrēsian)* or boldness, and the demonstration of hope in word and deed is the continuing mark of those who belong to Christ. It does not rule out periods of weak faith and struggle. Bruce comments, "Nowhere in the New Testament more than here do we find such repeated insistence on the fact that continuance in the Christian life is the test of reality." The true members of Christ's house are those who show the reality of their faith by holding on to courage and hope, even though they may waver at times. He further adds that stumbling from faith "is precisely what our author fears may happen with his readers; hence his constant emphasis on the necessity of their maintaining fearless confession and joyful hope" (1964:59).

To show his grave concern the author reminds them, in the second major warning passage of the letter, chapters 7—15, of the possibility of that apostasy which left thousands of Israelites dead in the wilderness. And this had even been under the leadership of Moses.

When Israel Failed to Enter Rest (3:7-11) Once again the writer draws from the treasury of the Psalms to support his warning. The be-

_____

3:7 Note again how concerned the writer is to identify Scripture as originating not with human beings but with God. The formula *as the Holy Spirit says* underscores the solemnity

ginning of Psalm 95 describes worship which is acceptable to God but closes with a flashback to the false worship of Israel in the wilderness. They had outwardly seen themselves as God's flock, but in their hearts they were hard against him and complained to Moses about their lack of water. The incident is recorded in Exodus 17:1-7. After God miraculously met their thirst by ordering Moses to strike the rock and bring forth water, Moses named the place Meribah (which means "quarreling,") and Massah (which means "testing"). Unfortunately, their attitude was not one of quiet trust in God, but one of fretful complaint and querulous challenge. This outlook was repeated many times (ten times, according to Num 14:22) throughout the wilderness wanderings until at last God said, "They are a people whose hearts go astray, and they have not known my ways. So I declared on oath in my anger, 'They shall never enter my rest' " (Ps 95:10-11).

God's anger is not lightly aroused. Their grumblings and murmurings were patiently endured over a span of forty years. On occasion God sought to make them aware of their ingratitude and rebellion by visiting them with deserved punishment (fire, plagues, quails and poisonous serpents). But he always offered repentance and recovery. Still, their complaints continued and their hearts gradually hardened until, at Kadesh-Barnea, when God commanded them to enter the land of Canaan and take it for their own, they rebelled and refused to go up. Finally, God spoke in anger and said, *"Their hearts are always going astray, and they have not known my ways. So I declared on oath in my anger, 'They shall never enter my rest.' "*

Note the reasons for his solemn oath: (1) They continually went astray *in their hearts.* Their inward life was askew. Rather than having a grateful spirit for astounding deliverances and limitless blessings, there was a settled attitude of complaint because everything did not go exactly as they desired each day. They saw themselves as deserving more than they were getting, and they resented it, not with an occasional outburst of displeasure, but with a constant harping that wore down everyone's nerves. (2) They had not learned God's ways. Over forty years, their real

of the warning and marks the writer's conviction that the Psalms are the very voice of God.

knowledge of God had not increased because their grumbling hearts blinded their spiritual eyes. A teachable spirit sustains a grateful heart. Centuries later Jesus would pray: "Now this is eternal life: that they may know you, the only true God, and Jesus Christ, whom you have sent" (Jn 17:23). This failure to grow in knowledge of God's ways is the very danger our author sees as a possibility for his own readers. He reminds them of this episode in Israel's history so they might heed its warning. Full apostasy is present when God says of anyone, *They shall never enter my rest.*

This is the first use of the word *rest* in Hebrews. This word describes the end of wandering and restlessness, and promises calmness and tranquility. Here it clearly refers to the land of Canaan and the promise of a settled state of peace and full supply. But, as we shall see, this Canaan-rest was a symbol, a shadow, of a greater rest available to the people of God in the future. The failure to correct a habit of grumbling and murmuring against God led over a million Israelites to such a hardened state of heart that they were unable to lay hold of the opportunity to enter the land of promise when they came to its borders. They perished at an average of almost ninety deaths a day, until the generation that left Egypt (except for Joshua and Caleb) had died out.

Don't Miss Your Opportunity (3:12-19) In verses 12-13, this example is now applied to all who read Hebrews. The writer's argument is: If unbelief kept Israelites out of the land of Canaan (a picture of God's rest), how much more serious is it today to give way to unbelief and thus miss the greater rest (the rest of justification and salvation). The warning is addressed to the whole assembly *(See to it, brothers, . . . encourage one another daily).* These phrases recognize individual responsibility to act *(that none of you has a sinful, unbelieving heart, . . . none of you may be hardened by sin's deceitfulness)* and describe accurately the terrible result of sin's hardening *(turns away from the living God).* Bruce

3:14 Kistemaker writes, "The parallel between Hebrews 3:6 and Hebrews 3:14 is striking. The imagery in verse 6 is of the house of God over which Christ has been placed as son and of which we are part. In verse 14 the same relationship is described as a sharing in Christ. And the courage and hope that we should 'hold on to' (v. 6) are identified as 'the confidence we had at first' (v. 14)" (1984:96).
3:18 Paul draws this same parallel in 1 Corinthians 10:1-5. In Egypt the Israelites all killed

puts it powerfully, "a relapse from Christianity into Judaism would be comparable to the action of the Israelites when they 'turned back in their hearts unto Egypt' (Acts 7:39); it would not be a mere return to a position previously occupied, but a gesture of outright apostasy, a complete break with God" (1964:66).

We who read this may not be battling with pressures to return to a previously held faith, but many church members today are content to live lives that are essentially no different than the lives of non-Christians around them. They easily forget Paul's plea, "Do not conform any longer to the pattern of this world, but be transformed by the renewing of your mind" (Rom 12:2). Also, "So I tell you this, and insist on it in the Lord, that you must no longer live as the Gentiles do, in the futility of their thinking" (Eph 4:17). All who ignore these words today are in great danger of repeating the ancient error of Israel.

For the first time in Hebrews the power of corporate faith is recognized with the words *encourage one another daily, as long as it is called Today.* It will be highlighted again in 10:24-25. Those who profess to share life in Christ are urged both to caution and encourage one another. This is done whenever it is needed *(Today* used eight times in Hebrews) and consists, not of stern rebuke, but loving admonition against a complaining spirit, and helpful illumination of sin's deceptive approach. "Sin is an extremely dangerous power confronting the believer. It always attacks the individual, much as wolves stalk a single sheep" (Kistemaker 1984:95). Its terrible danger lies in the deceptive ease by which it gradually hardens the heart, as it lessens the will's power to resist evil. As the first warning passage (2:1-4) dealt with the danger of drifting past truth, this one warns of the danger of failing to deal with a grumbling and complaining spirit.

Verses 14-19 recapitulate the warning from Psalm 95 and support the declaration of verse 14, *We have come to share in Christ if we hold firmly till the end the confidence we had at first.* This verse looks back to verse 6, "we are his [Christ's] house." Believers *share in Christ (metokoi,*

---

the passover lamb (foreshadowing the Cross of Christ). They all passed through the Red Sea (which Paul says corresponds to baptism). They all enjoyed the protection and guidance of the cloud and the fire in the wilderness (picturing the fatherly care of God today). And they all were fed by the manna and drank of the Rock (both symbols of Christ). But despite these outward signs, they never had really believed God but only sought to use him to avoid danger or unpleasantness. This is, sadly, the state of many today.

"become partakers of") through a dual relationship: "You in me, and I in you," that is, Christ dwelling in us as a Son in his own house; and believers dwelling in Christ, as sharers of his divine-human life. But this is made evident only by persevering as a Christian until the end of life itself! (See John 10:28 where Jesus says, "I give them eternal life, and they shall never perish"). Once again the *if* is descriptive, not conditional. *If we hold firmly . . . the confidence we had at first* envisages deliberate efforts made to renew faith and trust on a daily basis. As we read the Scriptures thoughtfully and closely every day, or when we pray regularly with and for one another, or when we worship with other believers in a shared experience of God's wonder and glory, when we serve people's needs out of love for Christ, we are doing the things that cause us to *hold firmly till the end the confidence we had at first.*

The rhetorical questions of verses 16-18 show how an outward façade of belief can be maintained while the heart is still unrepentant, and therefore unredeemed. It is possible to participate in and benefit from the great miracles of God, as the Israelites did who came out of Egypt with Moses (v. 16). Yet, despite such evidence, the heart can remain unchanged for a lifetime. God sees that inner hardness and warns continually against it until he is forced to judge it (v. 17). Note the growing stages of unbelief: general rebellion (v. 16); sin, punished by physical death (v. 17); and disobedience (Gk "being unpersuadable"—v. 18). The cause of this recalcitrance lies deeper than a wrong attitude or wrong behavior; it lies in a disobedient will. Therefore, the loss of promised blessing is traceable only and solely to long-continued unbelief (v. 19). This word *(apistian,* "disbelief") is the platform upon which the writer's more positive explanation of rest is founded. He gives us the other side of disbelief in chapter 4.

□ Greater Than Joshua (4:1-13)

Dreams of Utopia have haunted human minds for millennia. When Sir

---

Notes: **4:2** Many find it difficult to believe that the *same* gospel which is preached today (that is, the gospel of Christ) was also proclaimed to Israel in the wilderness. But note the two phrases *we have had the gospel preached to us* (v. 2) and *those who formerly had the gospel preached to them* (v. 6). No distinction is made in these uses of *gospel.* Also Paul states in 1 Corinthians 10:3, "They drank from the spiritual rock that accompanied them, and that rock was Christ." This implies an understanding on the part of some at least that the events

Thomas More, in 1516, wrote the book *Utopia,* he chose the name because in Greek it means "no place." Many attempts have been made in history to find or create such a place where life approaches perfection, but none has succeeded. Yet the dream has not faded, probably because it represents a vestigial human memory of something we once had and still yearn for, a greater Sabbath. On the seventh day of creation (*Sabbath* means "seven") God was said to have "rested from all his work" (Gen 2:2). This was not total inactivity, for God has been active throughout all history. It is probably best described as a rest of a perfectly functioning creation, as a mechanic rests from his work when his machine runs perfectly. That is what men have dreamed Utopia would be: a properly functioning society.

A Promise Requires a Response (4:1-2) In Hebrews 4:1 we are given the first hint that the promise of rest given to Israel envisaged more than entering the Promised Land. It is, he says, a promise which *still stands,* that is, was not satisfied by entering Canaan, but still exists at the time of his writing. Furthermore, his readers stand in danger of missing it unless they are careful. The Greek construction of the phrase *that none of you be found to have fallen short of it* indicates that wrong behavior, such as disobedience or long-continued grumbling, suggests the heart is unchanged and unbelieving. *Be found* refers to God's knowledge of the heart and his actions based on that knowledge.

In verse 2, we are given the reason for the Israelites' unbelief in the wilderness. Even though the gospel of God's deliverance from an evil heart was proclaimed clearly through the sacrifices, the tabernacle ritual and the preaching of Moses, it met with a lack of faith among those who perished. The writer will declare in 11:6 that "without faith it is impossible to please God." Without a personal response to the promise of salvation, no one may be saved. Declared many times in Scripture, this fact invalidates completely the teaching of universalism that everyone is

they experienced, the sacrifices they offered, the ritual they fulfilled, were all designed to teach them truth about a Redeemer who was, to the eyes of faith, their ground of atonement with God, though he had not yet appeared in history. Of course these same elements could be experienced mechanically, without faith, and were thus meaningless as far as personal salvation was concerned.

already saved by virtue of Christ's death and that God will reveal that to them at the end, no matter how they lived. This teaching ignores the need for repentance: turning from ungrateful rebellion to a thankful acceptance of God's provision. Romans 10:17 indicates that the gospel ("the word of Christ") has power to awaken belief in its hearers; if that belief is acted upon by a willing response (faith), it results in salvation (divine life imparted).

The Time for Response Is Today (4:3-7) In verses 3-10, we learn the full meaning of the word *rest*. First, it is a rest which believers of the first century (and today) can actually experience (v. 3). The writer uses the present, but not the future, tense, *we . . . enter that rest.* Jesus had declared, "Come to me, all you who are weary and burdened, and I will give you rest" (Mt 11:28). That is the same promise of rest which the writer, in verse 1, has declared *still stands.* If believed, it requires a response, for though the promise is still valid, so is the threat that follows: *Just as God has said, "So I declared on oath in my anger, 'They shall never enter my rest.' "* Now is the time to enter it (*today*— v. 7), and now is the time to lose it, if one tests God's patience too long.

Second, this true rest has been available since creation (vv. 3-4), and some who may not have entered Canaan could have entered God's rest still. God calls this rest *my rest.* This means not only does he give it, but he himself also enjoys it! He experienced rest when he ceased the work of creation, as recounted in Genesis 2:2-3. As we have seen, this does not imply subsequent idleness, for God continues to maintain his creation, as 1:3 attests. He is endlessly active in the work of redemption too, as Jesus declared in John 5:17. It does mean he ceased creating; he has rested from that work since time began. What that means for God's people will be made clear in verse 10. The third factor the writer stresses is that entering this rest must not be delayed. Again, he quotes Psalm

---

4:3-4 Did all those who died in the wilderness also perish eternally? Clearly not, since Moses, Aaron and Miriam are included in their number. Some, then, died before Canaan because they were unbelieving in relation to the picture of rest (Canaan) but did not perish eternally. But the majority were not only unbelieving about Canaan but also unbelieving

95:7, *Today, if you hear his voice, do not harden your hearts.*

Delay hardens the heart, especially when we are fully aware that we have heard the voice of God in the inner soul. Every shrug of the shoulder that puts off acting on God's urging for change, every toss of the head that says, "I know I should, but I don't care," every attempt at outward conformity without inner commitment produces a hardening of the heart that makes repentance harder and harder to do. The witness of the Spirit must not be ignored, for the opportunity to believe does not last forever. Playing games with the living God is not only impertinent, but also dangerous.

There is a line, by us unseen,
That crosses every path.
The hidden boundary between
God's patience and His wrath.

Today is a word of hope. All is not lost while today lasts. Though there has been some hardening, it can yet be reversed if prompt repentance is made. The situation is serious, though, for *Today* is never more than twenty-four hours long and that's all anyone is given at a time!

The Rest Obtained Is New-Creation Rest (4:8-11) Though Jesus is not compared here with Joshua in terms of relative greatness, it is apparent from verses 8-10 that the work of Joshua in leading Israel into the rest symbolized by the Promised Land was far inferior to the work of Jesus. He provides eternal rest to all who believe in him. The fact that God repeats his promise of rest through David in Psalm 95, centuries after Israel had entered Canaan, is used to indicate that Sabbath-rest is the substance and Canaan-rest but a shadow. There was an experience of rest for Israel in Canaan (from armed invasion, natural disasters, failure of crops) when they were faithful to God. But even at best that rest was outward and essentially physical, and could not satisfy the promise of rest to the human race which was intended from the beginning. The

about the redemptive provisions that pointed to Christ, and these we must presume to have been lost eternally.

4:10 I highly recommend Heschel 1975 for an insightful study on the sabbath from a Jewish viewpoint. Also Peterson 1987 has a most helpful chapter on a Christian pastor's observance of "sabbath" once a week.

author specifically states, *There remains, then, a Sabbath-rest for the people of God.*

In verse 10, we learn at last the nature of that rest. It means to cease from one's own work, and so, by implication, to trust in the working of God instead. In Ephesians 2:8-9 Paul asserts, "For it is by grace you have been saved, through faith—and this not from yourselves, it is the gift of God—not by works, [we are to rest from our own works!] so that no one can boast."

The use of the term *sabbatismos* ("Sabbath-rest") suggests that the weekly sabbath given to Israel is only a shadow of the true rest of God. Paul also declares in Colossians 2:16-17 where he lumps religious festivals, New Moon celebrations and sabbath days together as "a shadow of the things that were to come, the reality, however, is found in Christ." Thus *rest* has three meanings: (1) the Promised Land; (2) the weekly sabbath; and (3) that which these two prefigure, that cessation from labor which God enjoys and which he invites believers to share. This third *rest* not only describes the introduction of believers into eternal life, but also depicts the process by which we will continue to work and live, namely, dependence on God to be at work through us. "It is God who works in you to will and to act according to his good purpose" (Phil 2:13).

This is in many ways the lost secret of Christianity. Along with seeking to do things for God, we are also encouraged to expect God to be at work through us. It is the key to the apostle's labors: "I can do everything through him who gives me strength" (Phil 4:13). Also, "I have been crucified with Christ and I no longer live, but Christ lives in me. The life I live in the body, I live by faith in the Son of God, who loved me and gave himself for me" (Gal 2:20). Note, "I no longer live"—that is, I do not look for any achievement by my own efforts. Rather "Christ lives in me" and the life I live and the things that I do are "by faith"—that is, done in dependence on the Son of God working in and through me.

This makes clear that truly keeping the sabbath is not observing a special day (that is but the shadow of the real sabbath), but sabbath-keeping is achieved when the heart rests on the great promise of God to be working through a believer in the normal affairs of living. We cannot depend on our efforts to please God, though we do make decisions and exert efforts. We *cease from our own works* and look to his working within us to achieve the results that please him. As Jesus put it to the apostles, "Apart from me you can do nothing" (Jn 15:5). They must learn to work, but always with the thought that he is working with them, adding his power to their effort. That is keeping the sabbath as it was meant to be kept!

Learning to function from a position of rest is the way to avoid burnout in ministry or any other labor. We are to become "colaborers with God," to use Paul's wonderful phrase. This does not mean that we cannot learn many helpful lessons on rest by studying the regulations for keeping the sabbath day found in the Old Testament. Nor that we no longer need time for quiet meditation and cessation from physical labor. Our bodies are yet unredeemed and need rest and restoration at frequent intervals. But we are no longer bound by heavy limitations to keep a precise day of the week.

Paradoxically, we read in verse 11 the exhortation to *make every effort to enter that [sabbath] rest.* Of course, effort is needed to resist self-dependence. If we think that we have what it takes in ourselves to do all that needs to be done, we shall find ourselves *rest*-less and ultimately ineffective. Yet decision is still required of us and exertion is needed; but results can only be expected from the realization that God is also working and he will accomplish the needed ends. This is also the clear teaching of Psalm 127:1, "Unless the LORD builds the house, its builders labor in vain. Unless the LORD watches over the city, the watchmen stand guard in vain." Human effort is still needed, but human effort is never enough.

Failure to expect God to act caused the disobedience of Israel in the wilderness, and a similar failure destroys thousands today. It is called overachieving now, but it is the cause for most of the breakdown of Christians under the pressure of stress or responsibility. Pastors and teachers particularly have often been taught that they are personally responsible to meet the emotional needs and to solve the relational problems of all in their congregations. Many sincerely attempt this but soon find themselves overwhelmed with unending demands and a growing sense of their own failure. Relief can come only by learning to operate out of rest and by sharing responsibility with others in the congregation whom God has also equipped with gifts of ministry.

God's Word Will Reveal the Problem (4:12-13) The subtlety of the temptation to self-dependence is highlighted by verses 12-13. The opening *For* strongly ties them to verse 11 since they explain what the Israelites who fell in the wilderness failed to heed. David asks, in Psalm 19:12, "Who can discern his errors?" The answer he gives in the psalm and that of the writer of Hebrews is the same. Only the Word of God, which is living and active and sharper than any double-edged sword, is capable of exposing the thoughts and attitudes of a single human heart! We do not know ourselves. We do not even know how to distinguish, by feelings or rationale, between that which comes from our souls (psyches) and from our spirits (pneumas). Even our bodily functions (symbolized here by *joints and marrow)* are beyond our full knowledge. Only the all-seeing eye of God knows us thoroughly and totally (Ps 139:1-18), and before him we will stand and ultimately give account.

The images the author employs in this marvelous passage are effective ones. Like a sharp sword which can lay open the human body with one slashing blow, so the sword of the Scripture can open our inner life and expose it to ourselves and others. Once the ugly thoughts and hidden rebellions are out in the open, we stand like criminals before a judge, ineffectually trying to explain what we have done. Yet such honest revelation is what we need to humble our stubborn pride and render us willing to look to God for forgiveness and his gracious supply.

Plainly, Scripture is the only reliable guide we have to function properly as a human in a broken world. Philosophy and psychology give partial insights, based on human experience, but they fall far short of what the Word of God can do. It is not intended to replace human knowledge or effort, but is designed to supplement and correct them. Surely the most hurtful thing pastors and leaders of churches can do to their people is to deprive them of firsthand knowledge of the Bible. The exposition of both Old and New Testaments from the pulpit, in classrooms and small group meetings is the *first* responsibility of church leaders. They are "stewards of the mysteries of God" and must be found faithful to the task of distribution. This uniqueness of Scripture is the reason that all true human discovery in any dimension must fit within the limits of divine disclosure. Human knowledge can never outstrip divine revelation.

The remaining verses of chapter 4 (vv. 14-16) properly belong with the subject of chapter 5 and will be considered there. Thus far we have seen that Jesus is far greater than any angel, eclipses Moses as the spokesman of God, and leads believers into a far superior rest than Joshua led Israel into. In chapter 5, we are introduced to the major theme of Hebrews: the high priesthood of Jesus. He is superior in every respect to the priesthood of Aaron, and encompasses a ministry which the Old Testament only faintly shadowed in the mysterious ministry of Melchizedek to Abraham.

□ Greater Than Aaron (4:14—5:14)

As I was writing this chapter, I was concerned about a young man whom I wanted to help grow in Christ. At the moment his Christian life was on hold, and though he listened patiently to what I told him, he seemed unwilling to make any changes or to take seriously what I was saying. I found myself feeling frustrated and uncertain how to proceed. There was much truth I was anxious to impart to him and I longed particularly to open his eyes to the enormous resources for help in times of temptation and pressure that were available to him from the daily presence of Christ in his life. But he seemed to be dull of hearing and unable to grasp the excitement and vitality of what I was portraying. I began to realize how the writer of Hebrews must have felt as he tried to help his readers grasp the full import of the high priestly ministry of Jesus.

In 4:14 he begins an extended discussion of that ministry, which will conclude at 7:28. The *therefore* which opens the discussion looks back to the previous verse (4:13), where the whole human race is viewed as totally vulnerable before the all-seeing eyes of God. Our writer probably has in mind Adam and Eve, when they suddenly became aware of their nakedness and sought to hide from God in the Garden. But believers in Jesus, though naked before God, do not need to hide, for they have an Advocate before the Father, even the Son of God himself. Now they can, in the words of 4:16, *approach the throne of grace with confidence.*

The Priest Who Can Truly Help (4:14-16) Jesus, as high priest, is both *great* and *has gone through the heavens.* This last phrase denotes his completed work of redemption and transcendent availability. The practical result of that availability is that there is no necessity for anyone to give up faith under the pressure of peril or persecution, for the help needed to stand is both sympathetically offered and fully effective. This offer of help from on high to any who struggle with the pressures and problems of life on earth is undoubtedly the most widely neglected resource for Christians. It proposes simply and clearly to meet every situation, not with human wisdom but divine—and not with merely human strength, but God's inexhaustive strength! History provides many examples of those who have tried this offer and found it eminently true. Yet despite this encouragement from the past and present, many believers look only for human help, and if it is not available, succumb quickly to discouragement, defeat, despair and even suicide. These verses are often quoted as part of a Christian's defense provision, but too often forgotten when actual times of trouble arrive.

The basis for our great high priest's sympathy is that he has fully shared our plight. The writer has already (2:17) reminded his readers that Jesus was "made like his brothers in every way" and that this was done "through suffering" (2:10). Now we are told that he *has been tempted in every way, just as we are.* As Adam and Eve before the Fall could be tempted even in their innocent state, so Jesus could feel the force of temptation to the full, though he remained *without sin.* He exceeds us in his awareness of the power of temptation. "Such endurance involves more, not less, than ordinary human suffering" (Bruce 1964:86). Only the sinless can experience the full intensity of temptation, for the sinful yield before the limit of temptation is reached. We may count on his sympathy for our feelings of pressure and constraint to evil, and be assured, as the psalmist says, "he knows how we are formed; he remembers that we are dust" (Ps 103:14).

For centuries, Christians have debated the question, Was Jesus not *able* to sin because of his deity, or was he simply able *not* to sin even though he fully shared our humanity? This question is, in my judgment, one of those issues about which no final answer can be given due to the limitations of human knowledge and the reticence of Scripture to speak. If

Notes: 5:4 The Mormons claim that their male members are priests of the order of Melchizedek and that their prophet, Joseph Smith, held both the Aaronic and Melchize-

unduly pressed, it falls under Paul's warning against quarreling about words, for such quarreling "is of no value, and only ruins those who listen" (2 Tim 2:14). What Scripture does reveal in several places (7:14) is that Jesus was *without sin*. With that statement we should be content. Luther once observed, "When the angels want a good laugh, they read the commentaries!" Let us not add to their laughter by quarrels over things beyond our knowledge.

The *throne of grace* to which we come for help is pictured by the mercy seat in the old tabernacle. That mercy seat, where God could meet with sinful humans because of the blood of sacrifice sprinkled upon it, is the throne of power in the universe from which grace constantly flows to needy suppliants. Mercy is the remission of deserved judgment, while grace is the supply of undeserved blessing. Both are needed by sinful believers such as we all are, and both are available to us when we come with confidence. We are loved as children and cherished as recipients of the great salvation won by the blood of our great high priest!

The Qualifications of a Priest (5:1-4) Chapter 5 continues the priestly theme by looking first, in verses 1-4, at the necessary qualifications to serve as a priest. They are fourfold:

1. He must be human, "selected from among men" since he "is appointed to represent them" before God (v. 1).

2. His ministry consists of offering "gifts and sacrifices for sins," as his major work solves the alienation created by human sin (v. 1).

3. He must "deal gently with those who are ignorant and going astray," and he can do so because of his own sense of weakness and sin (vv. 2-3).

4. He must be appointed to his priestly office by God. No one can make himself a priest (v. 4).

All these Aaron fulfilled, as did, with varying degrees of accomplishment, many of his successors in the priestly office. We tend to think of the Levitical priests as engaged only in rituals and sacrifices which were often virtually meaningless to the people. But if we read Leviticus and

dek priesthoods. But this is a wholly gratuitous claim since it rests on no objective appointment by God but only on a subjective assertion in which they take this honor upon themselves.

Deuteronomy carefully, we will see that such priests served in the place of modern psychologists and psychiatrists today. In explaining to the people the purpose of each offering, they would be dealing with problems of fear, insecurity, anxiety, guilt and shame. Thus they fulfilled an extremely important role in the nation's life.

The Credentials of Jesus (5:5-10) The writer now shows that Jesus, as a high priest, fulfills each of those qualifications, though he is of a different order than that of Aaron. The fourth qualification is mentioned first—the need to be appointed by God. That divine appointment was found in the words of Psalm 2, quoted once before in 1:5, *You are my Son; today I have become your Father.* This precisely identifies the one who will be made a priest *(my Son)*, and is immediately linked with the words of Psalm 110:4, *You are a priest forever, in the order of Melchizedek.* This first of eight mentions of Melchizedek in Hebrews stresses the right of Jesus to serve because his appointment came directly from God and is confirmed by Psalms 2 and 110.

The second qualification (to offer gifts and sacrifices for sins) is not mentioned of Jesus here, possibly because it has been described already in 2:17. This will be dealt with extensively in chapters 8 and 9, particularly in 8:3. That Jesus met this credential in full is the major theme of Hebrews and is, therefore, taken for granted in this demonstration of his priestly qualifications.

But Jesus' fulfillment of the third qualification (to feel his own weakness and sins) is described in the words of verses 7-8. These strange verses explain how a sinless person could nevertheless feel his own weakness and sins. The major commentators agree that they describe the experience of Jesus in the dark shadows of Gethsemane. There—with only Peter, James and John nearby—he experienced a protracted period of excruciating torment of spirit which found expression in groanings ("If it be possible, Father, let this cup pass") and streaming tears, and ended in a terrible sweat, almost like blood.

There is a great mystery here. Jesus seems to face the experience with puzzlement and deep unrest of heart. For the first time in his ministry, he appeals to his own disciples for help, asking them to watch and pray for him. He confesses being deeply troubled in his spirit. Each of his three prayers questions the necessity for this experience and each is addressed *to the one who could save him from death*. Luke tells us that before the third prayer an angel was sent to strengthen him. Perhaps this is what the words of 5:7 refer to, *he was heard because of his reverent submission*. His cry to the Father was one of such desperate need that the Father answered by strengthening him through an angel. But when the angel had finished, the third and most terrible experience began.

The author implies that Jesus faced the emotional misery which sin produces: its shame, guilt and despair. He felt the iron bands of sin's enslaving power. He was oppressed by a sense of hopelessness, total discouragement and utter defeat. He is anticipating the moment on the cross when he would be forsaken of the Father, since he would then be bearing the sin of the world *as though it were his own*. The very thought of it crushed his heart as in a winepress. No sinner on earth has ever felt the stain and shame of sin as he did. He understood exactly the same feeling we have (in much lesser degree) when we are angry with ourselves and so filled with shame and self-loathing that we cannot believe that God can do anything but hate us for our evil. Jesus knows what that is like. He went the whole way and took the full brunt. We will never pass through a Gethsemane as torturous as he did. He saw our sins as his own, and thus fulfilled beyond any other priest's experience the ability to deal gently with other's sins since he was so fully aware of the sense of personal defilement sin leaves.

This also explains the unusual words of 5:8, *Although he was a son, he learned obedience from what he suffered*. There in Gethsemane he learned how it feels to obey when such obedience only promises further pain. He could and did add to his prayers, "yet not my will, but yours be done." Thus Jesus learned obedience when every fiber of his being longed to escape. He had gladly been obedient to the Father all his life. In Gethsemane it was hard, excruciatingly hard, for him to accept God's will, just as it often seems hard to us to obey it. But this is because we are impure, not pure. Nevertheless, even though he was a son who loved to obey his Father, yet he *learned* obedience the hard way through his experience in Gethsemane.

Verses 9-10 take us to the cross. Having learned obedience in Gethsemane, Jesus is now perfectly qualified to become at once the sin offering and the high priest who offers it. This anticipates the clause of 9:14, "through the eternal Spirit [he] *offered himself* unblemished to God." This perfect sacrifice, offered by the perfect priest, entirely supersedes the Aaronic priesthood and is again designated by God as of *the order of Melchizedek*. The phrase appears five times in Hebrews and becomes the subject of the epistle from 5:6 to 7:28. It is the Melchizedek priesthood that is described by 2:18: "Because he himself suffered when he was tempted, he is able to help those who are being tempted." In view of this help so easily available, why do we insist so strenuously on obtaining only human help? The mutual assistance of others like ourselves is scripturally valid and often helpful, but it was never intended to replace the help available from our great "Melchizedek." Let us go boldly and much more frequently to our high priest who sits on the throne of grace, ready and able to help.

Come, ye disconsolate, where'er ye languish,
Come to the mercy seat, fervently kneel.
Here bring your wounded heart, here tell your anguish,
Earth has no sorrows that heaven cannot heal!

The Spiritual State of the Readers (5:11-14) The paragraph from 5:11 to 6:3 turns aside for the moment to examine the spiritual condition of the readers of this epistle. Verses 11-13 describe their immature state; verse 14 shows them what they should be; and 6:1-3 tells them how to get there. There will follow, in 6:4-8, the third major warning passage of Hebrews, and in 6:9-20, the writer lifts his readers to a new level of hope based upon the oath and promise of God given to Abraham. He then will resume the discussion of the Melchizedek priesthood in chapter 7.

It has been quite evident thus far in Hebrews that the pastor's heart of the author has been deeply troubled over the spiritual state of some of his readers. Twice he has warned them at some length that they are in danger of repeating the unbelief of the Israelites in the wilderness and failing, therefore, to enter into the spiritual rest which they had been promised. Once again he confronts them with their perilous state.

5:11-12 A similar condition existed in Corinth where, in 1 Corinthians 3:1-3, Paul calls his readers "mere infants in Christ." He sees them as true believers (as the "in Christ"

They are *slow to learn,* he declares, and because of this dullness, he has difficulty in explaining to them the extraordinary advantages of the Melchizedek priesthood of Jesus. If they had been growing as they should, they ought by now to be able to pass the great truths of the faith along to others. They would no longer be learning *elementary truths of God's word* for themselves but could be *teachers* of those coming after them. The high priestly ministry which Jesus wants them to learn represents an advance on the introductory truths of the Christian faith. But instead of responding to his exhortations they seem to require those basic truths to be explained to them again. At best, they are spiritual infants who need to be taught over and over the elementary truths as a baby needs to be fed milk and is not ready for solid food. At worst, they are not Christians at all, but are like many of the Israelites in the wilderness. They also are in danger of failing to act in faith on the teaching they have received. Fear that this may be their condition is what leads the author to issue the solemn warning of 6:4-8, though in 6:9, he indicates that he does not yet believe they are all in such a fearful state.

The cause of their immaturity is clearly described in 5:13. They are *not acquainted with the teaching about righteousness.* Commentators differ as to whether righteousness here refers to conduct or imputed worth. Hughes opts for the latter view, describing it as "the teaching about righteousness which is fundamental to the Christian faith, namely, the insistence on Christ as our righteousness (1 Cor. 1:30, 2 Cor. 5:21) as opposed to self-righteousness or works-righteousness" (1977:191). Ignorance of having a righteous position in God's eyes already through faith in Christ has been the cause of much useless laboring to earn righteousness through the centuries. It invariably produces a form of legalism which tries to earn "brownie points" with God to gain his acceptance. The dullness which does not understand the divine program that leads to right conduct manifests its ignorance by being unable to "distinguish good from evil." But those who, by persistent obedience to the truth, are able to grasp such *solid food* will give evidence of it in wise and wholesome conduct. They will identify evil as evil, even when it

indicates) but says they are acting as "men of the flesh." It is difficult to tell the difference when their behavior is worldly and their learning listless.

looks good, and follow good because it is good, even when it looks evil.

How do Christians train themselves to be able to understand the teaching about righteousness? The steps are the same in any age. (1) Begin with truth you already know but have not been obeying. Does God want you to stop some activity you know to be wrong? Does Scripture exhort you to change your attitude, forgive someone, reach out with help to another? No further light will be given until you begin to obey the light you already have. (2) Review the promises of God for help from on high to obey his word, for example, Hebrews 2:18; 4:14-16; 2 Timothy 2:7. (3) Claim those promises for yourself, do whatever you need to do, and count on God's grace to see you through the consequences. (4) Follow this procedure whenever you become aware of areas of your life and thinking that need to be changed. This is the *constant use* which will enable one to grow and to handle the *solid food* of the teaching about righteousness. Paul, in Ephesians 4:14, says, "Then we will no longer be infants, tossed back and forth by the waves, and blown here and there by every wind of teaching and by the cunning and craftiness of men in their deceitful scheming."

Since understanding and practicing the truth of the high priestly ministry of Jesus leads believers to such maturity, it is obvious that it is one of the most important truths of Scripture and also one which every Christian should seek diligently to grasp and practice.

☐ Repentance Can Be Impossible! (6:1-20)

Life presents a thousand examples of the need to act on knowledge before any benefit is received. It is not enough to know a telephone number; if you want to talk to someone, you must dial the number. It is not enough to know the price of an object; if you want it, you must pay that price. It is not enough to know where India is; if you want to see it, you must go there. So it should not seem strange that the writer of Hebrews insists that to know Jesus you must receive him by faith and obey his teaching.

The unfortunate chapter division at this point tends to minimize the opening *Therefore* of chapter 6. Our author does not propose to teach his readers again *the elementary truths of God's word* though he has told them their dullness seems to require it. They already know the teaching; what they need now is personal commitment to it. This can only be achieved by going on to those actions of faith that produce maturity. For this reason he urges them to leave the *elementary teachings about Christ* and go on from words to applications. *Elementary teachings* is not a reference to regeneration, but means introductory information that could lead to regeneration.

Leave These Elementary Teachings (6:1-3) The rudiments he asks them to leave consist of six matters under two heads: (1) *the foundation of repentance from acts that lead to death, and of faith in God;* and (2) *instruction about baptisms, the laying on of hands, the resurrection of the dead, and eternal judgment.* These transitional truths lead from Jewish beliefs and practices to a full sharing in Christ. Though Bruce takes them as a Jewish list and others as Christian, the truth is they are both, as Bruce concedes that each "acquires a new significance in a Christian context" (1964:112). The point is that they do not represent anything but the barest beginnings of Christian faith. It is necessary to go from the knowledge of these initial truths to experiences which actually draw upon the priestly ministry of Jesus for this is what would lead them from head knowledge to heart response.

This rudimentary foundation is easily recognizable as the same one which Jesus and the apostles preached, namely, "repent and believe." Repentance is a permanent change of mind which results in right behavior ("Produce fruit in keeping with repentance"—Mt 3:8). The change they needed was to cease trusting in *acts that lead to death* (a phrase which is repeated in 9:14) or *useless rituals,* as the NIV alternatively translates. R. V. Tasker describes the result as "an abandonment of the attempt to obtain righteousness by seeking to obey the precepts of a lifeless moral code" (quoted by Bruce 1964:113). After turning from lifeless works (repentance), a positive action of *faith in God* must be taken. This recalls for us Paul's word to believers in Thessalonica: "You turned to God from idols to serve the living and true God." Repentance and faith are two sides of the same coin. They form the essential foundation upon which one may enter the Christian life.

Still, certain *instruction* in important doctrines was carried over from Old Testament teachings. This instruction falls into two sets: *baptisms* and *laying on of hands,* and *resurrection of the dead* and *eternal judgment.*

The first set touches upon the beginning of the Christian life; the second set speaks of its final events. Together they bracket Christian doctrine, involving both impartation of life and accountability of experience.

It is evident from the ministry of John the Baptist that Christian baptism emerged from the Jewish practice of ritual ablutions or washings. This would explain the unusual plural here (from *baptismos* used of Jewish ablutions, rather than from the more common *baptisma* which is employed for Christian baptisms). It may, however, be an oblique reference to John's teaching in 1 John 5:7-8, "For there are three that testify: the Spirit, the water and the blood; and the three are in agreement" which does tie water baptism with the Christian teachings of Spirit and blood. The point the writer wishes to make is that baptism is an initiatory rite and must not be regarded as fulfilling all that a Christian is expected to know or do.

The laying on of hands was widely practiced in the early church, sometimes for the imparting of the Holy Spirit (Acts 8:17), sometimes for healing (Acts 28:8), sometimes for ordaining or commissioning (Acts 13:3). Though borrowed from Judaism, its Christian usage would need to be explained to the new convert. It is an act of identification, tying the individual to either the activity of God or that of the body of Christ. This, too, represents a beginning and not an end.

The doctrine of *resurrection* is central to Christianity though not to Judaism. It was taught in the Old Testament (Is 26:19; Dan 12:2) and was important to the Pharisees (Acts 23:6), but its central position in the New Testament demanded further instruction and repeated exposure to the testimony of apostles and other eyewitnesses to the resurrection of Jesus. Since his resurrection is an essential element of the Melchizedek priesthood, it would be especially important that Christian converts be fully informed on this matter. The Pharisaic view of a resurrection at the end of time was nothing more than a mere introduction to this great theme.

The theme of judgment to come is also clearly taught in the Old Testament (Is 33:22; Gen 18:25). The figure of the Son of Man, who approaches the Ancient of Days to receive authority to judge (Dan 7:9-14), would most certainly be identified as Jesus to any scribe from a Jewish background. The author will refer to such judgment in 9:27, but the full development of this theme awaits the recognition of Jesus as the one who speaks from heaven (12:25) before the terrible shaking of the heavens and the earth.

This foundation and accompanying instruction could, if appropriated by faith, bring a Jew to new life in Christ. This would not be difficult to accept since it was based upon truth already taught in the Law and the Prophets. But though some among these Hebrews knew these truths intellectually, they gave little indication in their behavior that they had combined them with personal faith (4:2). The combination of the word about Christ with individual faith should have produced a Spirit-born vitality and enthusiasm which would make it delightfully easy to instruct them in the wonders of the Melchizedek priesthood. But since this élan is so visibly absent the writer must warn them that something is seriously lacking. It is dangerous to stay forever on the foundation; in fact, it is impossible. If they are not willing or able to move on to more mature understanding, they are in grave peril of losing what they already have, and that irretrievably! Growth in truth is something all Christians (note the *we* in v. 3) must do, *God permitting.*

Surely God would permit all of us to go on to maturity in the Christian life whenever we wished to do so! Or would he? This is the very question raised by the words *God permitting.* It seems to parallel the quotation in 3:11, "So I declared on oath in my anger, 'They shall never enter my rest.' " The unbelieving Israelites in the desert wanted to enter into Canaan, and, presumably, into the spiritual rest which Canaan symbolized. But they could not, for God would not permit it! Hence they must continue to wander in the wilderness till all were dead. Far from being a polite cliché or pious wish, these words *God permitting* form the fulcrum on which the warning of verses 4-8 turns.

The Danger of Knowledge Without Faith (6:4-8) This solemn warning marks one of the great theological battlefields of Scripture. Here the clashing proponents of Calvinism and Arminianism have wheeled and charged, unleashing thunderous volleys of acrimony against one another, only to generate much heat and little profit. The Calvinists, mindful of the doctrine of the perseverance of the saints (eternal security), seize upon the words *It is impossible . . . if they fall away, to be brought back to repentance.* "These cannot," they say, "be truly regenerated Christians, no matter how strongly the descriptive phrases of verses 4-5 seem to imply they are, for otherwise they would not fall away into irremediable apostasy."

On the other hand, the Arminians focus on the descriptive phrases and say, "It is impossible to portray true Christians any more powerfully and accurately than is done here; therefore, since they are said to fall away it is clear that regeneration can be lost after it has been obtained." A third group of interpreters insist that the question of eternal salvation is not in question here at all, since it is only a matter of urging new Christians on to further understanding of their fellowship with Christ.

As in the case of many clashes over Scripture, there is truth in different views. We are helped here by viewing the readers not as a homogenous group who must all be classified in one category or another. Rather, they are a mixed assembly, among whom were many genuine believers needing a degree of prodding to go on in their experience of truth. There were also some who professed faith in Christ but who gave no evidence in their behavior or attitudes that they were truly regenerate. This is the case in many churches today and has been so in every generation of believers from the first century on. No matter what careful expedients are employed to make sure that all church members are born again, it is almost certain that there is no congregation which is not just such a mixed multitude as the writer of Hebrews addresses. The ratio of true believers to apparent believers may vary widely, but since we cannot distinguish these by observation (or even careful testing), we must view these warnings as applying to us all.

Just how far religious experience can go and yet still fall short of regeneration is described by five phrases in verses 4-5. Let us look at them one by one. First is, *those who have once been enlightened.* Some of the early church Fathers linked this enlightenment with baptism, but that only identifies the effect with the cause. It plainly means an intellectual understanding of God's redemptive actions. The light of the gospel can be received

---

Notes: **6:4-8** A possible harmonizing of the Calvinist and Arminian views surrounding this passage may be found in the appendix. Henrichsen argues that the passage is not about eternal salvation at all, "In summary, the writer is saying that when a Christian falls into sin, it is impossible for him to be renewed through another conversion experience, because that would be equivalent to 'crucifying the Son of God all over again and subjecting him to public disgrace' " (1979:78). This interpretation would mean that it is impossible to treat the Savior so disgracefully, but that is just what the writer of Hebrews is warning his readers

without leading to baptism, but those who were baptized normally did so because they understood the truth about Jesus and his atonement and wished to avail themselves of its privileges. The *once* likely means "once for all" (Gk *hapax*), indicating that enlightenment cannot be repeated since a full understanding admits of no improvement. One sees this in the *epignōsin,* "full knowledge," of 10:26. But though knowledge is prerequisite to faith, it does not always indicate that saving faith is present.

The second description is that they *have tasted the heavenly gift.* The gift can be the Holy Spirit (2:4) or Jesus himself (Jn 4:10; 2 Cor 9:15), since both come from heaven. The mention of the Spirit in the next phrase seems to indicate the gift here is Jesus. Some commentators see this "tasting" as referring to the sacrament of the Lord's Supper, which identifies its elements as the body and blood of Jesus. Those who do have saving faith would surely observe this sacrament, yet it is quite possible to participate in baptism and the Lord's Supper without actual faith. Even if the reference is not to the Eucharist, it is still true that one can have much knowledge of Jesus and even have "tasted" of his blessings, without personal commitment to him (Jn 2:23-25).

The third distinctive, *who have shared in the Holy Spirit,* seems at first glance almost conclusive that these are true Christians. Paul's admonition "If anyone does not have the Spirit of Christ, he does not belong to Christ" marks the presence of the Spirit as the seal of a regenerated life. But there are other ministries of the Spirit that precede those of indwelling. One can become a sharer in or partaker of the Spirit by responding for a time to his drawing power intended to lead one ultimately to Christ. The translation "shared" implies something done in company with others, and may well be linked with the "laying on of hands" referred to in 6:2 (Kistemaker 1984:159). This would envision a group response to the gospel, as we see in many evangelistic rallies today, but it does not mean that all who so respond exercise saving faith. Since enlightenment and tasting are also min-

against doing. The passage, in this view, becomes only a hypothetical case which has no basis in reality.

6:4 Some have made the point that Jesus' tasting of death (2:9) clearly describes a full and complete death. Therefore, they argue, tasting the *heavenly gift* must mean an actual participation in the life of Jesus. But "taste" (Gk *geuomai*) is not always used in this way. In Matthew 27:34 it refers to Jesus' tasting the wine that was offered him on the cross but refusing to drink it. Thus here and in 6:5 "tasting" may indicate something only partial.

istries of the Spirit, they join the others as true of those who have traveled for a ways on their journey to faith, but who have not necessarily arrived.

A fourth mark of spiritual progress is to *have tasted the goodness of the word of God.* Since it is by the "living and enduring word of God" that men and women are born again (1 Pet 1:23), it is necessary to hear it first, and then "taste" its goodness. The readers of this epistle had done this, but there is no indication in this phrase that they have responded with personal faith. Some very likely have, but others have stopped short of the goal. And *this* arouses the concern of the writer.

The last, and fifth, advantage possessed by these Hebrews is that they have tasted *the powers of the coming age.* Hughes rightly says, "These powers may confidently be identified with the signs, wonders, and miracles mentioned earlier in 2:4 as accompaniments of the preaching of the gospel" (1977:211). These miracles were predicted in Isaiah 35:5-6 as accompanying the appearance of God among his people:

Then will the eyes of the blind be opened

and the ears of the deaf unstopped.

Then will the lame leap like a deer,

and the mute tongue shout for joy.

Jesus plainly saw himself fulfilling these words (Lk 7:22). It is apparent from these words in Hebrews that, eventually, in the divine program they would be manifest at both the first and second comings of Jesus. They belong primarily to the coming age, which is clearly not the new heavens and earth; these miracles of restoration will not be needed in that perfect day. They will be seen, finally, in the kingdom age when the prophet's picture finds its complete fulfillment. But the "taste" which many of these readers had had in the time of Jesus and the apostles was unconvincing evidence even to their own eyes. Like the Israelites who murmured in the wilderness, despite the miracles of supply they witnessed, these also failed to "share in the faith of those who obeyed" the word they heard.

Simon Magus (Acts 8:9-24) serves to illustrate the possibility that some

6:6 Hughes states, "The tenses of the Greek participles are significant: the aorist participle *parapesontas* indicates a decisive moment of commitment to apostasy, the point of no return; the present participles *anastaurountas* and *paradeigmatizontas* indicate the continuing state of those who have once lapsed into apostasy: they keep on crucifying the Son of God and holding him up to contempt" (1977:218). Some have understood the latter part of this verse to be a temporal statement ("It is impossible to renew them again unto

who experience such convincing proofs can nevertheless fall short of saving faith and turn away into apostasy. He professed belief in Jesus, was baptized and yet was severely rebuked by Peter because his "heart was not right before God." He was still a "captive to sin." Even more to the point is Judas, who walked and talked daily with the Lord, heard his superb teaching, witnessed many miracles and was himself sent out to minister in the power of God. But Jesus called him "the son of perdition" and "a devil" (Jn 6:70). Judas did not receive salvation and then lose it. Despite his enormous exposure to truth and grace, it is plain that he resisted personal conversion and at last turned away from eternal life to a sad and eternal death.

Verse 6 describes the grim result of turning back to unbelief after receiving the full enlightenment provided. Repentance is the gateway to eternal life, as many Scriptures make clear. After being brought by the Spirit-given blessings of verses 4-5 to the very edge of repentance, those who fall back into unbelief cannot be brought to that same place again, since nothing more could be added to that which proved insufficient before. Their state is now hopeless. As Bruce cogently observes, "God has pledged Himself to pardon all who truly repent, but Scripture and experience alike suggest that it is possible for human beings to arrive at a state of heart and life where they can no longer repent" (1964:124).

What blocks their way of return is that they have put themselves into the position of those who deliberately refused Jesus' claim to be the Son of God and forced him to the shame and humiliation of the cross. The NIV *because to their loss* does not translate the Greek *heautois* well. "To themselves" (KJV) or "on their own account" (RSV) is better. That is, they fall away deliberately, unwilling to separate themselves from those who actually condemned Jesus to be crucified. Their hearts are hardened in flintlike determination to have things their own rebellious way.

Verses 7-8 illustrate their situation exactly. The rain that falls from heaven corresponds to the enlightening blessings of verses 4-5. If the

repentance *while* or *so long as* they crucify to themselves the Son of God") rather than a causal one ("It is impossible to renew them again unto repentance *because* they crucify . . ."). Bruce says of this, "To say that they cannot be brought to repentance so long as they persist in their renunciation of Christ would be a truism hardly worth putting into words" (1964:124).

seed of the word of God is truly present in the soil (the hearts of men and women), the rain causes fruitful crops to grow, fulfilling the blessing intended by God. But where the word of truth, though heard, has been rejected, the rain can only quicken that which is already in the soil (thorns and thistles), and continued rain will only make matters worse, not better. Such fruitless land will merit the ultimate cursing of God and be finally given over to burning. Such a scenario parallels the condition Jesus describes of certain branches of the true vine which do not abide in him, and are therefore cut off and gathered into the fire and burned (Jn 15:2, 6).

Consistently throughout Scripture those who are genuinely Christ's do not fall away into apostasy. Thus Paul reminds the Philippians that the God who began a good work in them would complete it on the day of Christ. What our author fears is that there may be among his readers many who claimed to be Christians, perhaps witnessed for him, participated in the church, yet have refused to repent. Turning back from the light they have perceived, they prove to be enemies of Christ and not a part of the people of God at all!

Good Works Prove Faith Is Real (6:9-12) Having issued this warning, the pastor's heart of the writer expresses reassurance and encouragement in verses 9-12. Though some among them deserve his sobering caution, nevertheless he does not see them all in this dangerous state. It is clear that he sincerely believes that the larger part of his readers are truly saved and only need exhortation to diligence and patience. Their works of love and support to other believers strongly testify to their genuine faith, for as James declares, a faith that does not result in works is dead! (Jas 2:26).

Verse 11 states again the truth found everywhere in Scripture: The only reliable sign of regeneration is a faith that does not fail and continues to the end of life. It may at times falter and grow dim as it faces various trials and pressures, but it cannot be wholly abandoned, for Jesus has promised, "I give them eternal life, and they shall never perish; no one can snatch them out of my hand" (Jn 10:28).

One wag has observed, "If your faith fizzles before you finish, it's because it was faulty from the first!" I recall once receiving a phone call from a young new Christian who said, "I've decided to give up being a Christian; I can't handle it anymore." Knowing him well, I said, "I agree. That's probably what you ought to do." There was silence on the line for a moment, and then he said, "You know I can't do that!" And I said, "No, I know you can't." And he couldn't—and he didn't!

The Promise and Oath of God (6:13-15) True faith by nature awakens hope. In verses 11-12, the author urges the Hebrews to learn how to nurture faith and make their hope sure. The role models for this nurturing are the patriarchs, notably Abraham. Abraham's faith flourished because it fastened upon two facets of God's dealings with him: God's promise and his oath. A promise of many descendants was given to Abraham while he was still in Haran, recorded in Genesis 12:1-3. It was repeated when he arrived at Shechem (Gen 12:6-7) and reiterated on several occasions after that. Supported by these renewed promises, Abraham waited for twenty-five years until he was one hundred years old when Isaac was finally born. When Isaac had grown into young manhood, God commanded Abraham to offer Isaac as a sacrifice on Mount Moriah, now called the Temple Mount in Jerusalem. At the last moment, God stopped Abraham's hand. And after this dramatic act of Abraham's faith, God renewed his promise of many descendants and confirmed it with an oath (Gen 22:17). Since this oath appears in verse 14 and then is followed by Abraham waiting patiently to receive what was promised, it seems to refer, not to the birth of Isaac which had occurred many years before, but to the birth of Jacob who would be the father of the twelve tribes from which Israel sprang. Abraham was still living when Jacob and Esau were born to Isaac and Rebekah. So Abraham's faith, grown through the years of waiting, led at last to the fulfillment of his hope that he would have a line of descendants through whom all nations would be blessed. That hope found its ultimate fulfillment in Jesus, who said of Abraham, "Your father Abraham rejoiced at the thought of seeing my day; he saw it and was glad" (Jn 8:56).

The Anchor of the Soul (6:16-20) The author now applies this to his readers, in verses 16-20, by declaring that God, in his eagerness to convey to men and women of faith the total trustworthiness of his word, condescended to the human practice of adding a solemn oath to the promise he had given. Perhaps many today have had the experience of being put under oath in a courtroom or before a notary public. It is sobering to realize that any attempt at lying after the oath has been taken will result in punishment. Before the law, a mere promise to tell the truth is not enough—an oath must be taken. With God, of course, his promise is just as reliable as his oath—he *cannot* lie because his whole nature is truthful. But because he *wanted to make the unchanging nature of his purpose very clear* to any who seek his help, he condescended to add to his promise a solemn oath. So by these *two unchangeable things in which it is impossible for God to lie,* the readers of this letter, and we who share it with them, are greatly encouraged to take hold of the hope offered. Since God cannot lie to us, and actually confirmed his promise with an oath, let us, as the writer says, be *greatly encouraged.*

What, specifically, is that hope? It is the Melchizedek ministry of Jesus, as verses 19-20 make clear. He has already entered heaven on our behalf and stands ready as a great high priest to impart comfort, strength, forgiveness, love, joy and peace to any who flee to him for refuge in time of trouble. Like an anchor which holds a boat steady in the midst of a storm, he can sustain and steady us when we are battered and beaten by life. He can do this *forever* since he is not an Aaronic priest who can only minister for one lifetime, but a priest after the order of Melchizedek, who ministers in the power of an endless life! An old hymn catches the thought well:

We have an anchor that keeps the soul,
Steadfast and sure while the billows roll.
Anchored to the rock which cannot move,
Grounded firm and deep in the Savior's love.

The author of Hebrews pictures our faith entering the sanctuary in heaven where Jesus sits upon the throne. There it lays hold of his mercy and grace so fully that we are held fast, as though by a great anchor, against the beating waves of trouble and doubt. Held steady in the midst of trying circumstances, we grow in the certainty of our hope of glory. With these encouraging words of hope, he introduces the grand theme of his epistle: the new priesthood which operates on the basis of a new covenant and makes possible a fruitful life of faith in a faithless and hostile world.

□ Our Melchizedek (7:1-28)

Imagine this scenario. You are working as a junior executive in a large, well-known and prosperous firm. Your boss calls you in one day and commends you highly for the quality of your work and suggests you are being considered for a prestigious new position that will involve a handsome salary increase. But, he suggests, there is one possible hindrance. Your Christian convictions are well known and have been generally respected. But the new work will require a more liberal attitude toward certain ethical decisions you will need to make. You will be asked to overlook certain legal requirements and shade the truth somewhat in working out various business deals. The job is yours if you are willing to flex a bit, but it will go to someone else if you refuse. What will you do? Who will help you make a decision that will maintain your integrity in this pressure of temptation?

Transfer this scene from the twentieth century A.D. to the twentieth century B.C., the time of Abraham. Abraham has accomplished a remarkable and widely effective feat—with only 318 followers he successfully repelled an invasion of Palestine by a great coalition of the superpowers of that day. He has released many prominent citizens whom the invaders had captured and was returning home with wagons loaded with the treasures of Sodom which he had recovered. The grateful king of Sodom wishes to reward him by making him rich and giving him a position of honor in the lascivious lifestyle of Sodom. What would Abraham say? To whom should he turn for counsel?

Before he arrives at Sodom, Abraham is met at Salem (now Jerusalem) by its king and priest, Melchizedek. There he is refreshed physically and morally by the ministry of Melchizedek who greatly strengthens Abraham to resist the subtle appeal of the king of Sodom. In gratitude for this timely help, Abraham gives Melchizedek a tenth of the plunder he has won, and when the king of Sodom makes his offer, Abraham is fully prepared to say no! It is this incident that forms the historic basis for the commission of God, given centuries later through David in Psalm 110 to the Messiah, "You are a priest forever, in the order of Melchizedek."

The unfolding of the meaning of the Melchizedek priesthood of Jesus is the goal toward which the author has been aiming ever since 2:17, where he first uses the term *high priest* with reference to Jesus. This mysterious Melchizedek is mentioned in the Old Testament only twice, yet our author sees him prefiguring the most important ministry of Christ to his people today. The chapter establishes Melchizedek's historic identity; his precedence and superiority to the Levitical priesthood; the consequent need for a radical replacement of the Law; and the remarkable advantages which the Melchizedek ministry affords. These themes are little noted or understood in the average church today but desperately needed if the church (or the individual Christian) is to confront the world with power and grace.

Who Was Melchizedek? (7:1-3) The typology of the event recorded in Genesis 14:18-20, where Abraham returns from his conquest of four invading kings and is met by Melchizedek at the Valley of Shaveh (probably the valley of the Kidron at Jerusalem), is explained by the writer in verses 1-3. Melchizedek was both a king and a priest, and so is Jesus! Melchizedek blessed Abraham, refreshing and strengthening him with bread and wine. So Jesus strengthens and refreshes those who come to his throne of grace for help (4:16). Abraham paid a tithe (ten per cent) of all his goods to Melchizedek as an acknowledgment of his position as priest of the Most High God. So believers are to acknowledge Jesus as the one who has bought us with a price, and to recognize we are no longer owners of ourselves or all we possess (1 Cor 6:19-20)!

Melchizedek was both king of righteousness (the meaning of his name) and king of peace (Salem means peace). So Jesus is the sovereign possessor of both righteousness and peace, and can dispense them to his own as gifts which they may continually have but can never earn! Finally, as Melchizedek appears in the record of Scripture with no men-

Notes: **7:3** Resurrection is the visible manifestation of eternal life, and John declares, "This life is in his Son" (1 Jn 5:11). Eternal life is apart from time, having no beginning or ending, and thus Jesus is properly described as *without beginning of days or end of life.*

For those interested in alternative views of the identity of Melchizedek, Hughes (1977:237-45) supplies a survey of Jewish and Christian thought on this subject through the centuries. Early Jewish thought regarded Melchizedek as a heavenly being, but the rabbis of the first century sought to identify him with Shem, the oldest son of Noah, to counteract the Christian view of him as a type of Christ. The early Christian writers for the most part objected to this as invalidating the claim of Hebrews that Melchizedek was "without genealogy," since the genealogy of Shem was well known.

Certain Gnostic cults taught that Melchizedek was a theophany of the Holy Spirit, while a later sect saw him as a preincarnate appearance of the Son of God. But Epiphanius (d.

tion of his parents or his children (though he was a normal human being, certainly with parents and probably with children)—nor does the Genesis account mention his birth or his death—so the risen Jesus has neither beginning nor end, nor a human parentage to his resurrected life. Therefore, he can serve as a merciful and faithful high priest forever (7:23-25)! Though some commentators have viewed Melchizedek as a preincarnate appearance of Christ, the phrase *like the Son of God* seems to militate against that. "Melchizedek thus was the facsimile of which Christ is the reality" (Howley 1969:552). To a modern congregation, this passage should be presented as a vivid picture of the help which is available for believers today from our great high priest who can give us righteousness and peace from within if we "come to the throne of grace to receive mercy and find grace to help us in our time of need."

The Melchizedek Priesthood Superior to the Levitical (7:4-10)
This focus on Melchizedek in Hebrews is intended to bring out the inherent superiority of the priesthood of Jesus to that of the Aaronic line, the descendants of Levi, who had ministered in the tabernacle and temple throughout Jewish history until the Hasmonean line was established. Verses 4-10 argue this superiority further. The author argues that Melchizedek is greater than Abraham, the great-grandfather of Levi, for four reasons:

1. Though the Levitical priests also received tithes from their Israelite brethren, their descent from Abraham marked their priesthood as less important than that of the one to whom Abraham tithed, namely Melchizedek (vv. 5-6).

2. Abraham was blessed by Melchizedek at the time of their encounter,

403) responded to that suggestion, saying, "If Melchizedek resembles the Son of God, he cannot at the same time be the same as the Son of God; for how can a servant be the same as his master?"

Scrolls found in Cave 11 at Qumran speak of Melchizedek as the coming great Deliverer of the Jewish remnant and equate him with the archangel Michael. If the readers of Hebrews were being attracted to the teachings of the Dead Sea sect, the author's treatment of Melchizedek would go far to correct misunderstanding of his importance. The Latin father Jerome states that the reliable church authors he had consulted on the identification of Melchizedek included Irenaeus, Hippolytus, Eusebius of Caesarea and Apollinaris, who all viewed Melchizedek as a human being. Most of the Reformers followed this view, though modern commentators have occasionally made other identifications.

and normally the lesser is blessed by the greater (v. 7).

3. Levitical priests all eventually die but, as Psalm 110:4 declares, the One who ministers in the order of Melchizedek lives forever (v. 8).

4. In some genetic sense, Levi, great-grandson of Abraham, actually also paid tithes to Melchizedek since he was at the time a part of Abraham's reproductive system which would produce Isaac, then Jacob and, ultimately, Levi (vv. 9-10). This line of argument may seem strange to our Western, individualistic mentality, but it reflects the more accurate realization of the links between generations, and the fact that we are governed more by our ancestry than we often believe. The same line of argument is found in Romans 5:12, where Paul declares that the whole human race has sinned in Adam, and that death is therefore universal because of Adam's sin. He sees the whole human race as potentially present in Adam when Adam sinned, and therefore participating with him in the aftermath of that sin.

The Aaronic Priesthood and Law Replaced (7:11-19) The argument of verses 11-19 constitutes a bold, and even radical, declaration by the writer. This section asserts unequivocally that the death and resurrection of Jesus has introduced a new and permanent priesthood that brings the Levitical priesthood to an end and, with it, the demise of the law of Moses. It is important to note in verses 11-12 that the law was originally given to support the priesthood, not the other way around. The priesthood and the tabernacle with its sacrifices were the means God employed to render the sinful people acceptable to himself. They constituted the shadow of Jesus in the Old Testament. Then the law was given with its sharp demands to awaken the people to their true condition so that they might avail themselves of the sacrifices. This agrees fully with Paul's statement in Romans 5:20 and Galatians 3:19-23 that the law was a teacher to lead to Christ (represented in Israel by the tabernacle and its priesthood).

To suggest that either of these venerable institutions (the priesthood

---

7:18-19 A problem recurrent in Hebrews arises from the clear teaching that animal sacrifices could not and did not remove the sin of the offerer. How then could a holy God have any part with yet unholy people? The answer is that when an Old Testament believer offered a sacrifice with a trustful and repentant heart, God would, in grace, view it as pointing to the death of Jesus and the believer's act of faith would, like that of Abraham, be "counted

and the law) were inadequate and needed change was to assault Judaism in its most sacred and revered precincts. But that this was the teaching of Christians from the beginning is seen in the savage charges hurled at Stephen, and later Paul, when they engaged certain Jewish leaders in religious dialog. See, for instance, Acts 6:14, where Stephen's opponents testified, "We have heard him say that this Jesus of Nazareth will destroy this place [the temple] and change the customs Moses handed down to us."

If (as some Jews thought) perfection could be achieved by means of the law and priesthood, the author asks in verses 11-14 what need would there be for God to announce a new priesthood as he did through David in Psalm 110? He clearly implies that the Melchizedek priesthood of Jesus was in the mind of God centuries before the Levitical priesthood and the law. These latter could never have produced the perfection of character which God required. His argument is that if the priesthood of Jesus has now replaced that of Levi, then the law of Moses must also be replaced because it is the natural accompaniment of the Levitical priesthood. Sacrifices and offerings would no longer be useful for covering sins, and the law which awakened sin must pass as well. It is a powerful declaration which would arouse immediate antagonism among certain Jews, as indeed history has shown. He further indicates Jesus' priesthood as being different from the Aaronic in that those priests all belonged to the tribe of Levi while Jesus came from the tribe of Judah. Since Moses said nothing about that tribe serving as priests, it is plain that the present priesthood of Jesus does not rest on Moses or his law. It is the ultimate provision for dealing with human sin and weakness toward which the Levitical priesthood and law pointed.

One reason the law and the priesthood could not accomplish the perfection God requires is given in verses 15-18. Levitical priests were ordained only if they could prove their ancestry from Levi, and must be replaced at death by another of the same line. By contrast, Jesus holds

---

for righteousness." Sometimes the personal faith of the offerer did see beyond the animal blood to the promised sacrifice which God would offer. David evidently saw this for he cries to God, "You do not delight in [animal] sacrifice, or I would bring it; you do not take pleasure in burnt offerings" (Ps 51:16).

the Melchizedek priesthood forever because he possesses *an indestruct-ible life*. It is not merely endless; by its very nature it cannot be ended! As Psalm 110:4 declares, it is "forever." Nor does it require specific an-cestral descent. Any man who fit the qualifications could serve and, as we have seen, Jesus is the only man who fulfills all the qualifications. So for the fourth time, Psalm 110:4 is quoted, *You are a priest forever, in the order of Melchizedek*. All the limitations created by sinful humanity are removed and a perfect priest now serves who works effectually and lives forever.

The glorious result of this is stated in verse 18: the *former regulation* (the priesthood and the law) is set aside as weak and useless since it cannot cleanse from sin or provide power to obey. A *better hope* is brought in to replace it which will do what the law and the priesthood could not do—enable us to *draw near to God*. In 10:22 the writer will exhort his readers to do this very thing, since it is now fully possible because of the Melchizedek priesthood of Jesus.

The Levitical priesthood was ended because its purpose was fulfilled. It is, and always has been, *weak and useless* to go further and actually remove sin. That was done and perfectly done in the sacrifice of Jesus. But removal of sin is not the only thing sinners need—they also need a continuing supply of refreshment, strength and wisdom to enable them to live in a hostile world. This is now supplied through the Melchizedek priesthood. Kistemaker states the truth well: "Through his unique sacri-fice he [Jesus] fulfilled the responsibilities of the Aaronic priesthood, and through his endless life he assumes the priesthood in the order of Mel-chizedek" (1984:196). The "picture" of the Old Testament is fulfilled accurately and the *better hope* of the new covenant is introduced.

The Guarantee of a New Covenant (7:20-28) Many items on the market today carry with them a warranty or guarantee. It constitutes the manufacturer's promise that the item sold will fulfill the buyer's expec-tations. Our author now sees God's oath, uttered in a fifth reference to Psalm 110:4, as the guarantee that the better hope available from the new Melchizedek will be delivered as promised. No such oath was given in establishing the Levitical priesthood. As in 6:17, where God's oath to Abraham is said "to make the unchanging nature of his purpose very clear to the heirs of what was promised," so again God's oath in Psalm 110:4 reassures believers today that God has provided a merciful, faithful, fault-less, competent and sympathetic high priest. He will meet their needs for cleansing, courage, wisdom, and personal support in danger or sorrow. This "stress-management program" is fully and continuously available. Also he *will not change his mind* about it, for, indeed, he offers no other alternative! The old covenant will no longer work and no secular or pagan solution to the problem of sin and spiritual immaturity is acceptable.

This thought introduces the word *covenant* for the first time in Hebrews. In verse 22 the new covenant promised in Jeremiah 31:31-34 is linked directly with the Melchizedek priesthood of Jesus. The word *enguos* ("guarantee"), used only here in the New Testament, describes Jesus' relationship to that new covenant. Verses 23-25 point out the way he guarantees, not merely mediates, the covenant. A mediator would offer the covenant, but it would be up to the believer to receive it. A guarantor, however, sees to it that the covenant is fulfilled, even though the believer resists and stumbles at times. It is because Jesus lives forever that he can guarantee ultimate results. No Levitical priest could compete in that aspect of priesthood since their personal death ended their ministrations. But Jesus has a permanent priestly office and the conclusion naturally follows: he can save totally, completely, all who come to God through him. As Jude 24 declares, they shall be presented before his glorious presence without fault and with great joy! He does this by continually interceding in prayer for them before the Father. Paul likewise recognizes this in Romans 8:34, "Christ Jesus, who died—more than that, who was raised to life—is at the right hand of God and is also interceding for us."

Bruce (1964:155) suggests we have a sample of that intercession in our Lord's prayer for Peter (Lk 22:32) and in his high priestly prayer of John 17. In answer to those prayers, all believers are being shaped and polished by the Spirit into the likeness of Christ (2 Cor 3:18). That perfect likeness is gradually growing within us, along with the daily manifestations of imperfection and evil which come from the "old man" still resident in our fleshly bodies. But at the resurrection all that old life ends forever and only the perfection of Christ remains, formed in us by the Spirit. We are saved *completely* by the work and prayers of Jesus.

In the closing words of the chapter, verses 26-28, the author summarizes the qualities which make Jesus, our Melchizedek, the perfect fulfillment of the needs of sinful humans living in a confused and God-ignoring age.

1. As to his person, he was and is holy—that is, morally flawless, perfectly balanced, without impurity or lack.

2. He also was, and is, blameless, as perfect outwardly as he is holy inwardly.

3. In his dealings with others, he was, and is, pure; for he is without stain, untouched by the defilement around him.

4. He is set apart from sinners, though not in any isolative sense, for he kept company with the disreputable as well as with the respected. He came to call sinners, not the (self)righteous, to repentance. But he is eternally the Son of God, while we are sons of God only by redemption. Peter instinctively recognized this separation when he cried out to Jesus upon seeing the miraculous catch of fishes, "Go away from me, Lord; I am a sinful man!" (Lk 5:8).

5. Jesus' final personal qualification is that he is exalted above the heavens. This is confirmed by the statement of 1:3, "He sat down at the right hand of the Majesty in heaven." No higher authority can be found in all the universe. He is, in the words of Paul, "far above all rule and authority, power and dominion, and every title that can be given, not only in the present age but also in the one to come" (Eph 1:21).

As to his work, his sinlessness means he does not need to sacrifice for his own sins, but nevertheless he offered himself as a sacrifice, which he did *once for all.* It is of continuing and eternal merit. The Levitical system of animal sacrifices is ended, and with it, the regulations for priesthood. The oath of God, found in Psalm 110:4, now establishes the Son of God as high priest forever in the order of Melchizedek.

Such then is our Melchizedek, God's provision for help in our daily life, incomparable in greatness, inexhaustible in resource, infinite in patience, infallible in wisdom and interested in all that concerns us. We can now understand much more clearly why the writer of Hebrews longed to impart information about the Melchizedek priesthood of Jesus to his readers and bewailed their dullness and slowness to learn (5:11-12). But it leaves us with the question, Are we any more alert than they? Do we actually avail ourselves in this modern world of the provision for the help which this chapter describes? Let us each answer as best we can!

☐ The New Covenant (8:1-13)

On the night in which he was betrayed, Jesus took a cup of wine, passed it to his disciples and said: "Drink from it, all of you. This is my blood of the covenant, which is poured out for many for the forgiveness of sins" (Mt 26:27-28). With those words and that symbolic action, he borrowed the phrase used by Moses when he took the blood of an animal, sprinkled it on the people and said, "This is the blood of the covenant that the LORD has made with you in accordance with all these words" (Ex 24:8). The contrast was deliberate. Moses used the blood of an animal; Jesus used wine as a symbol of his own blood. Moses spoke of the covenant of the law; Jesus alluded to the new covenant of grace. Moses spoke of God's words which provided for the partial covering of sins so God could remain with his people; Jesus promised the actual remission of sins so God could live within his people forever. It is that excellent new covenant which chapters 8—10 of Hebrews now expounds.

The Royal High Priest (8:1-6) We have already seen that a covenant rests upon a priesthood, not the other way around. It is the priesthood that makes the covenant effective. Just as the old covenant of law could never be more effective than the priesthood it represented, so the new covenant of grace can never do more than the high priest from whom it flows. So, in 8:1-2, the writer turns his spotlight on the central figure again: *The point of what we are saying is this: We do have such a high priest.* He is not only a priest but a king, and he sits on the throne of universal authority. Doubtless, this refers again to Psalm 110. His priesthood is a royal one which gives him, as Jesus himself declared, "all authority in heaven and on earth" (Mt 28:18). Furthermore, it is exercised not in a tabernacle or temple on earth, but in what might well be called the "control room" of the universe, the heavenly sanctuary, the true tabernacle.

The mention of a *true tabernacle set up by the Lord, not by man* refers back to 3:5-6, where Christ as Son serves in a greater house than Moses served in. As we saw there, "we [believers] are his house" of which the tabernacle erected in the wilderness is but a picture or type. *True* is not used in contrast to something false, but means "original," in contrast to that which was a copy. Here the symbols of God's throne and a true sanctuary are combined to describe the supremacy of the new covenant over the old. Both symbols are located *in heaven* and identified in some way with Christ's house. These relationships will become clearer as the author moves into the next two chapters.

Verses 3-6 declare again that the offering of gifts and sacrifices is essential to the work of a priest (5:1), but the sacrifice Jesus offered went far beyond anything being offered in the temple on earth. His was not that of a mere animal but of a living person as the writer has just declared in 7:27. Note that he ties the priestly ministry then going on in the temple with that prescribed for the tabernacle of old, and speaks of both as *a copy and shadow of what is in heaven.*

Stress is laid on the instruction which God gave to Moses about building the tabernacle in the wilderness exactly to the pattern given him on Mount Sinai. This temporary tabernacle was only a copy of something eternal and central to all things, a heavenly tabernacle which Moses saw. In Revelation 8:3-5 and 11:19, this heavenly sanctuary appears again, but there it is called a temple. This lends justification to the view of many that the writer of Hebrews saw the temple in Jerusalem as the legitimate successor to the tabernacle in the wilderness. The tabernacle/temple passed away, as it was intended to do, but the truth it was meant to teach abides forever. That truth will be developed further in Hebrews 9, but here it introduces the extensive quote from Jeremiah 31 which describes the new arrangement for living which our great high priest both mediates and guarantees. It is called the new covenant. This new provision of God for his people is twice described in verse 6 as *superior (kreittosin,* "better"), because it is built on better promises. Those promises are listed by Jeremiah as threefold: an inner understanding of truth, an intimate relationship with God and an absolute forgiveness of all sins.

The Better Covenant (8:7-13) The quotation itself is found in Jere-

Notes: 8:5 The typology of the tabernacle has been greatly neglected by modern scholars, though obviously the writer of Hebrews makes much of it, and many nineteenth-century commentators treated it seriously. If, as this passage suggests, it is the key to understanding the present ministry of Jesus in the inner lives of his people, it deserves far more study than it is now receiving.
8:8-12 There is no inherent need to pit amillennialism against premillennialism in these

miah 31:31-34. So important does the writer consider this that he partially quotes it again in 10:16-17. As he has done before (4:8; 7:11; 8:4), he argues from a logical consequence: *if there had been nothing wrong with that first covenant, no place would have been sought for another.* Two things were found wrong with the covenant of the law. First, the people did not fulfill its conditions, despite their initial avowal to do so (Ex 24:3). Second, it was not sufficiently powerful to motivate them to obedience since it was not written on their minds or hearts (Calvin 1949:187). Israel's failure is reflected in the phrases *God found fault with the people* and *they did not remain faithful to my covenant.* This new covenant is declared to involve a different relationship between God and his people from that under the old covenant, precisely because the old covenant did not keep the people from failure and God had to turn away from them.

Therefore, in verses 10-12, the gracious provisions of the new covenant are detailed. It must not be ignored that in both the original passage from Jeremiah and here, it is clearly stated that the new covenant is to be made *with the house of Israel and with the house of Judah.* Both verse 8 and verse 10 refer to a *time* when this occurs. Since the two divisions of the kingdom (Israel-Judah) are distinguished, this is clearly a literal promise. Such a time will indeed come when the ancient divisions will be forgotten and Israel shall be one nation living in the land promised them. Ezekiel confirms this in Ezekiel 37:15-23. At that time, he states, God promises to cleanse them, and "they will be my people, and I will be their God," the very words used by Jeremiah as the main provision of the new covenant. This, too, is the substance of Isaiah's awed prophecy:

Who has ever heard of such a thing?
Who has ever seen such things?
Can a country be born in a day
or a nation be brought forth in a moment?

matters. Amillennialism is true when it metaphorically applies the literal promises made to Israel to the redeemed human spirit today. But that does not necessarily mean there will be no literal fulfillment to Israel. It is not an either/or situation, but a both/and! The promises to Abraham and David concerning the land and the throne have never yet been fulfilled in history, but will be when Jeremiah's vision of the new covenant applied to Israel is fulfilled, as Paul also envisaged in Romans 11:15 and 26-27.

Yet no sooner is Zion in labor
than she gives birth to her children. (Is 66:8)

New Testament support for a time when Israel will be saved is found in Paul's words, paraphrasing Isaiah 59:20-21: "The deliverer will come from Zion; he will turn godlessness away from Jacob. And this is my covenant with them when I take away their sins" (Rom 11:26-27).

Though the writer of Hebrews undoubtedly applies this new covenant to the church, those commentators who deny its future application to the nation of Israel ignore great areas of Old and New Testament prophecy. The basis for applying this passage to the church, though it is not stated in Hebrews, is Paul's declaration in Romans 15:4 that "everything that was written in the past was written to teach us, so that through endurance and the encouragement of the Scriptures we might have hope." And again, "These things happened to them [Israel] as examples [Gk *typikos,* as 'types'] and were written down as warnings for us, on whom the fulfillment of the ages has come" (1 Cor 10:11).

But whatever or whenever the application, the terms of the new covenant are exciting. First, *I will put my laws in their minds and write them on their hearts.* Every true Christian knows that when he or she was regenerated, a change occurred in their motivation. They found they *wanted* to do things they formerly did not want to do; for example, reading the Bible, or attending church, or praying and meditating. They found their reaction to evil in their own life was also different. What they once enjoyed without qualm, they began to be disturbed about and even to hate. They experienced at least something of the struggle which Paul so eloquently describes in Romans 7:15-19. This is the practical experience of the promise of the new covenant, to give a new and inner understanding of both good and evil. The laws of godly behavior are written on their hearts.

The second provision is equally remarkable: *I will be their God, and they will be my people. No longer will a man teach his neighbor, or a man*

8:13 In Galatians 3:25 Paul concludes a long section on the relationship of law to believers with these words: "Now that faith has come, we are no longer under the supervision of the law." This has been taken by some to mean that the Ten Commandments no longer are valid for Christians and serve no purpose in their lives. But in Romans 10:4 Paul states, "Christ is the end of the law *for righteousness* to everyone who believes"—that is, as far as obtaining righteousness is concerned, Christ is the end of the law (for law cannot make

his brother, saying, "Know the Lord," because they will all know me, from the least of them to the greatest. Every true Christian also knows the inner sense of belonging to God in a new way. God is no longer seen as a stern Judge, but a loving Father. Believers are no longer outside the community of faith as aliens or exiles. They are now members of a family. They discover that whenever other members of the family are met, they too know the Father just as they know him. This new intimacy with God and his children becomes the bedrock of emotional stability in the Christian's experience. Notice how John develops this in 1 John 2:9-14.

The new covenant's third provision is: *I will forgive their wickedness and will remember their sins no more.* This is, perhaps, the most difficult aspect for us to believe, for it forces us to do two difficult things: recognize that we do wicked things, and believe that God has already made ample provision to set aside that wickedness and continue treating us as his beloved children. Any sin called to our attention by our conscience needs only to be acknowledged to be set aside. Provision for God to do so justly rests on the death of Christ on our behalf, not on our sense of regret or our promise to do better. As Paul states in Romans 8:31, God is always *for* us, he is never against us. He does not ignore iniquity in us, but is merciful toward us. When we acknowledge it, there is no reproach—or replay—from him! We can live with a daily sense of cleansing by the precious blood of Jesus. That will do wonders for our sense of guilt or inadequacy.

The author's point in verse 13 is simply that when the new covenant takes effect, there no longer is any reason to rely upon the old one. This does not mean the law of Moses (the Ten Commandments) is done away with, for Jesus himself teaches that it will last as long as the heavens and the earth (Mt 5:18). What these words in verse 13 mean is that the law's work is finished when men and women come to Christ. It could not make them perfect, but they have now come to One who can! Since the

us righteous). But in other matters the law still serves believers, as Paul makes clear in 1 Timothy 1:8: "We know that the law is good if one uses it properly." He then goes on to cite many sinful acts and attitudes which the law helps us to discover within ourselves so that we may then acknowledge them and place them under the blood of Jesus which "purifies us from all sin" (1 Jn 1:7).

Aaronic priesthood under which the law was given has now been replaced by the Melchizedek priesthood of Jesus, there is no longer any need for the law to work its condemning work in a believer's life. "Therefore, there is now no condemnation for those who are in Christ Jesus" (Rom 8:1). Awareness of sin is now the work of the indwelling Spirit, not to condemn, but to restore us, when we repent, to useful and fruitful service.

Many commentators have pointed out that historically the phrase in verse 13 *what is obsolete and aging will soon disappear* may well point to an awareness on the author's part that the priesthood of Israel, the temple in which they served, and all the rituals and sacrifices of the law which they performed, were about to be ended by the overthrow of Jerusalem as Jesus had predicted. This seems to be additional evidence that the letter to the Hebrews predates A.D. 70.

In chapter 9, we will return to the tabernacle and its ritual that we may more clearly grasp the realities of the new covenant and the freedom it gives us to live in a pressure-filled, baffling and bewildered world by the power that flows from our high priest today.

□ The True Tabernacle (9:1-28)

In C. S. Lewis's well-known Chronicles of Narnia, he describes how several quite ordinary English children, while playing hide-and-seek, enter a quite ordinary English wardrobe. Pressing deeper into the familiar garments, they suddenly find themselves in a strange and mysterious land. Some such phenomenon occurs to those who think deeply about what Scripture says about that humble structure of skins and panels called the tabernacle. At first, all is factual, measurable and straightforward. But as we press deeper the walls silently move back, the commonplace begins to glow, and soon we find ourselves before the awesome throne of God in a heavenly temple, surrounded by myriads of worshiping angels, and watching the ritual of redemption through wholly transformed eyes.

Notes: 9:4 The manna would remind Israel of God's miraculous and loving care of them in the wilderness; the rod of Aaron would mark the Levitical priesthood as divinely instituted and far more important than any human provision; and the stone tablets of the covenant would speak of the holy character which God's people must continually measure themselves against. Together they spoke of God's love, God's redemption and God's holiness. These

This could well have been the experience of the apostle John which he records vividly in Revelation 4 and 5. Until A.D. 70, the rituals of the law were performed daily, weekly and yearly in the temple at Jerusalem. Yet the writer of Hebrews only obliquely refers to the temple. Rather, he centers his thought on the tabernacle which was set up by Moses in the wilderness according to the pattern shown him on Mount Sinai. As we have already noted, the writer sees the temple as a continuation of the tabernacle. That tabernacle was intended to hold such a central place in the life of Israel that Moses was warned not to deviate one iota from the pattern given him when he had it constructed. Everything about the building and its furniture was meant as a teaching tool by which supremely important truth could be conveyed.

The Furniture of the Tabernacle Described (9:1-5) As the author points out in verses 1-10, the typology of the tabernacle has great meaning for believers today since it depicts the eternal verities which Moses saw and which were associated with the new covenant and its priesthood. If we wish to understand that new priesthood and covenant, we must carefully study the tabernacle, both its structure and its rituals. This teaching would be readily acceptable to the readers of this treatise who came from Jewish backgrounds. The writer builds on this knowledge to unfold the great advantages of the new ministry.

The tabernacle had three main parts: an outer court, which was entered through a single gate and in which stood the brazen altar of sacrifice; the brass basin, or laver, used for the cleansing of the priests; and the skin-covered, rectangular building of the tabernacle proper. That building was divided into two rooms and separated by a curtain. The first room was called the Holy Place and contained the seven-branched lampstand (the Menorah), the table of showbread and the golden altar of incense. In verse 4, the writer places the altar of incense within the second room, the *Most Holy Place* (more literally in Hebrew idiom

find their counterpart in Christian experience: God's love for us initiates his redemptive activity (Jn 3:16); God's provision for us goes far beyond what any amount of human counseling or control can achieve (2 Cor 5:17); and God's sanctifying work within us produces at last a Christlike character that is fully acceptable to a holy God (2 Cor 3:18).

the "Holy of Holies"), because it was closely associated in worship with the ark of the covenant and its mercy seat. But the ark of the covenant actually stood alone behind the second curtain. In this Most Holy Place the ark of the covenant represented the dwelling place of God, visible in the Shekinah, or glowing light, which rested between the cherubim atop the mercy seat. Within the ark were Israel's most treasured possessions: the jar of manna which never spoiled (Ex 16:32); Aaron's staff which had sprouted and borne fruit when Aaron's priesthood had been challenged by the heads of the other tribes (Num 17:8-10); and the actual tables of the law which Moses had brought down from the mountain, written on by the finger of God (Ex 32:15).

The Meaning of the Ritual (9:6-10) Verses 6-7 remind readers that there was a special sanctity about the Most Holy Place and the ark of the covenant. No ordinary Israelite could ever enter the Holy Place where the Menorah, table of showbread and altar of incense stood, but the priests went in there daily to perform their ministrations. But even the priests could not enter the Most Holy Place and stand before the ark of the covenant. Only the high priest could do so, and then only once a year on the Day of Atonement (Yom Kippur). He must take with him a basin of blood from the goat which had been sacrificed on that day and sprinkle that blood on the mercy seat for his own sins and the sins of the people (Lev 16). The question which must come before us in reading this is, What did all this carefully prepared building, furniture and ritual represent? What was the reality of which all this was only a copy? Or, to put it most simply, What did Moses see on the holy mountain which he faithfully reproduced in a symbolic copy, the tabernacle? The answer to this is suggested by certain statements that follow, notably verses 8, 11, and 23-24. But the writer now states he does not want to be tied up with the details of the tabernacle's meaning but hastens to

9:8 A comparison of standard texts will indicate this:

KJV—"the way into the holiest of all was not yet made manifest, while as the first tabernacle was yet standing."

RSV—"the way into the sanctuary is not yet opened as long as the outer tent is still standing."

NEB—"so long as the earlier tent still stands, the way into the sanctuary remains unrevealed."

stress a most important point.

The levitical offerings had to be repeated continually—even the offering of the high priest on the Day of Atonement when he entered the Holy of Holies once a year. This endless repetition meant that nothing permanent was ever accomplished by the Aaronic priesthood. The central statement is verse 8 which declares what the Holy Spirit meant to say by this repeated sacrifice. Unfortunately, the verse is almost always badly translated. Most versions, like the NIV, take the last phrase as suggesting that while the tabernacle/temple was still existing, the way into the true sanctuary was not yet revealed. But that would be tantamount to saying that until A.D. 70, when the temple would be destroyed, there was no way of understanding how the death of Jesus had opened a new and living way into the true sanctuary, the presence of God. If taken in this way, it would give no meaning at all to the rent veil at the time of the crucifixion and no hope that anyone, before A.D. 70, had found salvation through the sacrifice of Jesus!

A better translation makes it all clear. The Greek phrase *eti tēs prōtēs skēnēs echousēs stasin* should not be rendered, "while the first tabernacle is still standing," but "while the first tabernacle still has any standing!" That indicates the writer is saying that the repeated sacrifices of the old covenant were meant by the Holy Spirit to predict a perfect sacrifice that was yet to come, but it could not be apprehended while still relying on the old way of access to God! In other words, the truth of the reality could not be grasped while one was yet clinging to the shadows. The first tabernacle had to lose its standing before the reality it prefigured could be apprehended.

This meaning is confirmed by the opening words of verse 9, *This is an illustration for the present time.* The old arrangement pictured the new, but the old proved ineffective, for it could not touch the inner, but only the outer, life. The veil that stood before the Most Holy Place

NIV—"the way into the Most Holy Place had not yet been disclosed as long as the first tabernacle was still standing."

Phillips—"the way to the holy of holies was not yet open, that is, so long as the first tent and all that it stands for still exist."

Hughes suggests this understanding in saying that *ekein stasin* goes beyond the meaning "to continue in existence." Following Teodorica, he says its force is "to have legal standing" or "official sanction" (1977:322).

constituted a barrier to the presence of God. All Israelites, who knew of that barrier, must have felt a continuing deep sense of personal uncleanness until the next year's Day of Atonement. Their consciences would know no relief, for they must feel separated from God until the yearly sacrifice could be repeated.

The tabernacle worship, with all the provisions of bread, incense, offerings—even the ornate building itself with its altars—was all a kind of religious play. It was meant to teach the people what was going on in their inner life and what was still needed to truly free them from sin's burden and give them unfettered and continuing access to the Living God. Their bodies could be rendered temporarily clean before God by the various ceremonial washings (v. 10), but their consciences remained defiled. Since they could find no heart-rest in the tabernacle ritual, they were being encouraged to look beyond the outward drama to what was important. But when Christ died and the veil of the temple was torn from top to bottom God was saying: "The time has come; the way of access is fully open; the need for pictures is over."

This has been the argument of Hebrews all along. To cling to the shadows of the past and not to move on to the clear light of the great reality in Christ is to put our whole eternal destiny at stake and, in fact, to be in danger of drifting into a total apostasy. Let the tabernacle and its ritual lose its standing in our eyes. Go on to the reality to which the Holy Spirit is pointing—the full forgiveness of sins of the new covenant and the resulting intimacy with God.

Those who today try to earn a sense of being pleasing to God by good behavior need to hear this lesson. Never knowing when they have done enough, they feel troubled and restive without any heart-peace and thus are often driven to extreme measures of self-punishment and despair. They need to cease from their efforts and trust in Christ's completed work.

9:11 In equating the human spirit with heaven, I do not mean to imply that the human spirit in which the Spirit of Christ dwells is equivalent with all that Scripture includes in the word *heaven.* I simply mean that there is an obvious correspondence between the two and that in the spirit we are in some sense living in heaven now (Eph 2:6).

Moses saw, of course, the whole person—body, soul and spirit (Gen 2:7; 1 Thess 5:23). This would explain the threefold division of the tabernacle. The outer court corresponds to the body; the Holy Place, to the soul; and the Most Holy Place, to the spirit. Even the furniture of the tabernacle corresponds to elements in us. For instance, the furniture of the Holy Place was the lampstand, the table of bread, and the altar of incense. If the Holy Place

The Application to Christians (9:11-14) The section from verses 11-14 confronts us anew with the question raised above, What is the reality of which the tabernacle was a copy? Verse 11 says it was a *greater and more perfect tabernacle . . . not man-made, . . . not a part of this creation.* Verse 24 adds, *he entered heaven itself, now to appear for us in God's presence.* We have already been given a clue to the meaning of this in 3:6, "For Christ is faithful as a son over God's house. *And we are his house."* He dwells within us as he said he would (Jn 14:23) and as Paul affirms (Eph 3:16-17). The fact that this house is also termed *heaven* is difficult for us to grasp, since we tend to think of heaven spatially. It is "up there" or "out there" or even in some distant part of outer space. If we would eliminate spatial terms from our thinking, we could come to think of heaven as simply another dimension of existence, as another realm of invisible realities just beyond our senses — in other words, the spiritual kingdom in which God, angels and even demons, function. What the Bible seeks to teach us, and what is difficult for us to apprehend, is that we too can function in this dimension. It is the dimension of our spirits. Thus, Paul can say, "And God raised us up with Christ and seated us with him in the heavenly realms in Christ Jesus" (Eph 2:6). Jesus tells us, "God is spirit, and his worshipers must worship in spirit and in truth" (Jn 4:24), and Paul adds, "He who unites himself with the Lord is one with him in spirit" (1 Cor 6:17).

All of this strongly suggests that what Moses saw on the mountain was the human person as we are meant to be, the dwelling place of God— the Holy of Holies. John tells us in Revelation, "Now the dwelling of God is with men, and he will live with them. They will be his people, and God himself will be with them and be their God." If that language sounds reminiscent of the promises of the new covenant described in Hebrews 8, it is no accident. God had this in mind from the very begin-

is the soul of man, these pieces would suggest the mind (lampstand), the emotions (bread as a symbol of social intercourse) and the will (altar of incense, which reflects the choices God approves). But Moses was shown that though God dwells in the human spirit and makes us different from the animals, we have no access to him because of sin. We are described as "dead in trespasses and sins" and said to be "alienated from God," "without God in the world." But Paul states the great truth of Hebrews 9 in these words: "But now in Christ Jesus you who once were far away have been brought near through the blood of Christ" (Eph 2:13).

ning, as David declares in Psalm 8: "You made him [human beings] a little lower than the heavenly beings and crowned him with glory and honor." These words, as we have seen, were quoted by the writer in 2:5-8 and to this, he appended: "Yet at present we do not see everything subject to him. But we see Jesus . . ." Jesus, *as high priest of the good things that are already here,* has found a way to repossess the human spirit and cleanse it with the "better sacrifice" of himself (9:23), and to dwell within forever by means of the eternal Spirit (9:14).

This view of the true tabernacle as the human person is also supported by Paul in his description of what awaits believers at death. "Now we know that if the earthly tent we live in is destroyed, we have a building from God, an eternal house in heaven, not built by human hands" (2 Cor 5:1). Here the phrase "not built by human hands" is the same as that in Hebrews 9:11 translated "not man-made." It is clearly a reference to the resurrection of the body. This would also explain the phrase *not a part of this creation* in Hebrews. Our humanity was not created as glorified already. A glorified body is an additional step which Adam did not know in his earthly existence and which would, therefore, be "not of this creation."

The point our author makes in 9:11-14 is that if the blood of goats and bulls and the ashes of a heifer offered in the tabernacle of old sufficed to cleanse the sins of those ceremonially unclean and to forgive the rebellions of the past so that the people were temporarily acceptable to God, how much more does the blood of Christ cleanse our consciences from sin's defilement today? They had only animals to offer in sacrifice, and it was necessary to repeat them again and again. But Christ offered only one sacrifice, not an animal but himself, and he did it *once for all.* This indicated its continuing, unbroken efficacy, which obtained not merely a temporary and outward cleansing, but *eternal redemption.* As we have seen, it is the conscience within which acts as a barrier to God's presence. Like Adam after the Fall, we tend to hide ourselves from God, fearing his judgment. Conscience cannot be rendered inactive by our

---

9:11-24 Hughes (1977:283-290) has a helpful excursus on the various interpretations of the terms *the true tent* and *the greater and more perfect tent.* These views include the humanity of Jesus, the human body, the church as the body of Christ, the souls of God's people, the literal heavens and simply the presence of God. All of these have elements of

will, though its voice can be muffled. It is only silenced when we see that God is not unhappy or angry with us. But since Jesus *offered himself unblemished to God* in our place, God's justice no longer makes demands upon us. We may, therefore, set aside useless rituals and so feel ourselves free in his presence to serve the Living God.

Jesus' Last Will and Testament (9:15-28) The passage from 9:15 through 9:28 takes a slightly different slant. Though the same term *covenant* is used as in verses 1-14, it is now treated more as a bequest being administered by a living executor after the death of the will-maker. However, Christ is seen both as the will-maker who dies, and the executor who administers the estate, just as he was both the offering for sin and the high priest who offered it. The phrase *For this reason,* which introduces verse 15, looks back to the close of verse 14, *that we may serve the living God.* The promised Messiah administers the new covenant to *those who are called* in order that they may be equipped to serve the living and true God. That equipping capability of the new covenant is called *the promised eternal inheritance.* We have already seen that it consists of an inner understanding of the nature of both good and evil; an intimate, Father-child relationship with God; and a total and continuing forgiveness of sins. This is the inheritance which our Mediator offers to us whenever we come to the throne of grace (4:16) to receive it by faith. Just as the heir of a fortune may draw from its resources at any time, so we are expected to draw from this great bequest, as it is now available to us after the death of the testator.

The last clause of verse 15 introduces the author's emphasis on the bequest, or *promised eternal inheritance,* flowing from the death of Jesus. Verses 16-17 argue that the covenant (viewed as a will) cannot take effect apart from the death of the will-maker. This principle is seen even in the first covenant (vv. 18-22) since Moses, having read the law to the people, took the blood of animals and sprinkled the scroll of the law, the people and everything connected with the service of the tabernacle

truth about them but suffer from the spatial concepts still included in them. The truth is, we do not know very much about the realm of spirit. This is probably what Paul means by his famous statement in 1 Corinthians 13:9-10, "For we know in part and we prophesy in part, but when perfection comes, the imperfect disappears."

(Lev 8:10, 19, 30). He thus indicated that the old covenant was based upon death—the death of animals. Without such a death, even the limited forgiveness provided for in the first covenant could not take effect, for *without the shedding of blood there is no forgiveness.* A striking scene is described in Exodus 24:8 when Moses sprinkled the blood upon the people. It was meant to impress on them that sin cannot be set aside, even by a loving God, without a death occurring. His judicial sentence, "the soul who sins is the one who will die" (Ezek 18:4), must be carried out. By sprinkling the blood of an animal on the people, Moses is saying that God would accept that substitution as a temporary reprieve until the true Substitute should come. The people must realize that sin is serious, since only death can relieve it. When the new covenant replaces the old, it not only removes sin through the death of Jesus but provides a new understanding and a new intimacy that make the service of God a delight and an enriching experience.

By contrast, the author stresses again the value of the death of Jesus. Verses 23-26 speak of the blood of Jesus as an infinitely *better* sacrifice than the animal deaths that purified the *copies of the heavenly things* contained in the tabernacle. Though the imagery here is drawn from the Day of Atonement, we must not think of Jesus as bearing a basin of his own blood into heaven to present it before the throne of God at his ascension, as some commentators have concluded. The rending of the curtain in the temple at the time of the crucifixion is ample evidence to indicate that the blood shed in the death of Jesus was the moment when full atonement for sin was accomplished.

The writer lays great stress on the contrast between the repeated offerings of the high priest in the tabernacle on the Day of Atonement and the one offering of Jesus upon the cross. Because of the infinitely superior nature of Christ's sacrifice, founded on his deity and sinless humanity, his one offering was enough for all time. He need not *suffer many times since the creation of the world* to do away with sin, but the one sacrifice of himself was sufficient.

_____

9:24 To adequately picture an event having many implications, such as the cross, required a multiplication of actions in the Old Testament which would not be necessary to duplicate in the reality. For instance, the Day of Atonement required two goats: one a scapegoat to be released into the wilderness, and the other to be slain and its blood

As we have already noted, the entrance, by faith, of Jesus into the spirit of a believer gives this person access to the heavenly reality which corresponds to the earthly Holy of Holies. That is where God now dwells (Jn 14:20, 23), and where our great high priest makes intercession for his own. He has no need to suffer and die again since his perfect sacrifice of himself completely satisfied every demand of divine justice. He can now sustain and support his people without any limitation on himself arising from their sins, since that has been settled forever in the once-for-all sacrifice of the cross. The phrase *the end of the ages* designates the present age as the last of a series. It marks the end of human history as we now know it and will terminate in the events which Jesus foretold would occur "at the end of the age" (Mt 24—25).

Throughout this section the emphasis of the writer has been on the uniqueness of Christ's death. Again and again he has called it "once-for-all" (*hapax* or *ephapax*). That thought comes to the fore again in verses 27-28. Just as any fallen human being is destined to die once for all time, with judgment awaiting beyond death, so Christ also died once for all time to deal with sin. For the many who trust in him, it is not judgment that awaits beyond their personal death. This judgment has been forever removed by the sacrifice of Christ. Instead, they may confidently expect that *he will appear a second time, not to bear sin, but to bring salvation to those who are waiting for him.*

This salvation points to the resurrection of the body. For them, the spirit has been regenerated already and the soul is *being saved* as Christ-likeness is formed in that believer (2 Cor 3:18). What yet awaits is the raising of the body so that the whole person becomes a dwelling place of God forever. This is the only place in the New Testament where the return of Christ is called a *second* coming. During his first coming, he dealt with the problem of human sin on the cross; at his second coming the full effect of that sacrifice will be manifested in the resurrection (or "transformation"—1 Cor 15:51-52) of the bodies of those who wait for him.

---

sprinkled within the Most Holy Place. Both actions were needed to depict the death of Jesus as both bearing sin away forever and cleansing believers from its defilement. Similarly, the dying of Jesus fulfilled both the offering of a sacrifice and the presentation of its blood by the high priest.

In these closing verses of chapter 9, the writer returns briefly to the thought of 2:5-9 and his view of Jesus as God's ideal human being, who rules over the world to come. That view of the final triumph of Jesus will appear again at the end of chapter 10, as the author concludes his survey of the privileges and possibilities of the new covenant. As always, the thought of the return of Christ raises the question Peter asked in light of such events, "What kind of people ought you to be? You ought to live holy and godly lives as you look forward to the day of God" (2 Pet 3:11-12).

□ Let Us Go On! (10:1-39)

It would be foolish indeed to prefer reading a cookbook to eating a good meal when one is hungry. Not that there is anything wrong with reading a cookbook—it can be very enlightening—but it is not very nourishing! Yet some of the original readers of Hebrews were doing something very much like that. They preferred to content themselves with the externals of faith—such as the law, the Aaronic priesthood and animal offerings—and to ignore the fulfillment of these things in the death, resurrection and ascension of Jesus. They wanted the cookbook rather than the meal!

As we have seen, the tabernacle in the wilderness, with its regulations and sacrifices, was an accurate and divinely drawn picture of the sacrifice of Jesus and the new arrangement for living which would be available to believers in Christ. But it could only describe these realities up to a point. It was both a comparison and a contrast.

I carry a picture of my wife in my wallet and, when I am away from home, I find it comforting to look at it. But it is quite inadequate, for it is not my wife, only a picture of her. I can look at it, but I cannot have a conversation with it. I cannot laugh together with it, and I cannot persuade it to cook any meals! It is an accurate representation of the real thing, but also a far cry from it. So the law and the tabernacle could never do for believers of any age what the living Christ can do. This is the continuing argument of the writer in chapter 10.

A Willing Sacrifice (10:1-10) A new aspect, however, is seen in chapter 10. The sacrifice of Jesus was one he came into the world prepared to make! It was no impulsive commitment on his part; he made it only after he had observed human misery. In verses 1-4, the author builds on a point he has made earlier—that the annual repetition of sacrifices in the old order indicated their inability to actually remove sins. Once again he uses a logical-deduction argument. Had they truly cleansed the conscience, there would have been no need to repeat them for the offerers; they would have seen themselves as cleansed from sin's defilement forever. But these sacrifices could not remove sin because they were based only on the death of animals.

The annual repetition did remind offerers that they were still very much sinners and still very much in need of an adequate substitute if their sin was ever to be removed. The sacrifices were but *a shadow of the good things that are coming—not the realities themselves.* A shadow indicates a reality, but has no substance in itself. I waited on a downtown street corner one day for a friend who always wore a Western hat. Suddenly I saw his distinctive shadow on the sidewalk and knew that he was standing just around the corner. I could not actually see him, but I knew he was there. So the offerings witnessed to the person of Christ and his sacrifice, though they were not that reality themselves. They were but his shadow that indicated he was soon to appear.

The *good things that are coming* are the equivalent of *make perfect* which the repeated sacrifice of the Day of Atonement could never achieve. To *make perfect* a sinner before God would be to have sin and its effects totally removed. These include not only the effects on the spirit and soul but the body also—regeneration, full sanctification and resurrection. Though resurrection awaits the final coming of Christ, nevertheless, full and continuing access to God, "without the constant necessity of removing the barrier of freshly accumulated sin" (Bruce 1964:227), was available by faith to every believer in Jesus throughout the believer's lifetime (Rom 5:1-2).

These animal deaths were unwilling, even unconscious, sacrifices of a lower and quite different nature and therefore inadequate substitutes for humans made in the image of God. *It is impossible,* says the author, *for the blood of bulls and goats to take away sins.* Isaiah had quoted God long before saying, "I have no pleasure in the blood of bulls and lambs and goats" (Is 1:11). Nevertheless, despite this limitation, through the deaths of many animals, one unchanging message was being pounded out. Every sacrifice declared it and every offering told the same story. It was burned in blood and smoke into every listening heart. The essential point for a God-approved dealing with sin in one's life was that a life be laid down. Every dying animal meant a life brought to an end. Sin was serious; it forfeited life. Unless the sin could actually be removed, the sinner must die. To save the sinner from such a fate, an equal and willing substitute must be found. Such a substitute the author now finds described in the words of Psalm 40.

Verses 5-7 quote Psalm 40:6-8 from the Septuagint. They describe, in words directly ascribed to Christ, his complete willingness to sacrifice himself to remove our sins. His was a self-giving life, not self-loving, as animal sacrifices were. Though there are different wordings here than the Hebrew text presents, nevertheless the central point is clear. Jesus saw himself described in the Suffering Servant passages of the Old Testament *(it is written about me in the scroll), and willingly set himself to fulfilling that role in his incarnation (Here I am. . . . I have come to do your will, O God).* Wholehearted obedience is the quality which God desires in sacrifices. He makes the point many times in the Old Testament, notably, in 1 Samuel 15:22; Isaiah 1:11-14; and Amos 5:21-22. As Morris rightly says, "God takes no delight in the routine performance of the ritual of sacrifice" (1983:91). Undoubtedly, he feels the same way about routine worship services today!

That none of his readers should miss this important point the writer takes pains to indicate clearly, in verses 8-10, the meaning of the quote from Psalm 40. He acknowledges that though God authorized the animal sacrifices of the past, he did not delight in them. Then he stresses the fact that Christ deliberately set himself to do the will of the Father, though he knew it would lead to pain and separation. Intimations of Gethsemane are certainly present in these words, though it was on the cross that they were fully carried out. Here the writer also declares that

Notes: 10:5-7 The major difference between the Septuagint and Hebrew versions lies in the term "a body you prepared for me," found in the Septuagint, and the words "but my ears you have pierced" in the Hebrew text. The Hebrew may be read as "my ears you have digged," that is "hollowed out," which would describe the creation of that part of the body. Thus the body prepared by God is symbolized by the creating of the ears, and is given back to him in obedient service (Bruce 1964:232). If we relate this latter phrase to the words

the death of Jesus, by fulfilling the will of the Father, completely replaces the provision of animal deaths which had provided some degree of forgiveness before. Finally, he announces the only possible conclusion: it is by the fulfillment of the will of God in the once-for-all sacrifice of Jesus Christ (note the double name, only here in Hebrews) that we (all believers) have been made holy. The Greek expression for *made holy* indicates action with a lasting effect. We have been made holy by the death of Jesus, and we remain holy even though we struggle with daily weakness and sin. This should be borne in mind when we come to the statement in 12:14, "without holiness no one will see the Lord." It is a holiness obtained by faith, not by self-righteous effort, and it is not lost by momentary failure. "There is now no condemnation for those who are in Christ Jesus!" (Rom 8:1).

A Complete Sacrifice (10:11-18) One peculiarity of the tabernacle was that it contained no chairs. The priests were not permitted to sit, but performed their ministries while standing. Our author maintains in verses 11-12 that this symbolically shows that their work was unfinished, so their repeated sacrifices could not finally remove sins. But when Christ had offered himself as a sacrifice *for all time,* he sat down at God's right hand (1:3; 8:1; 12:2) for two excellent reasons (vv. 13-14).

First, there was nothing left for him to do except to await the outworking of the salvation he had accomplished on the cross. This would, of course, involve his mediation of the new covenant and his intercession for believers. No further sacrifice of any kind was required or needed. Enough had already been done to deal with every form of sin or rebellion. He could remain figuratively seated until his enemies had been totally rendered impotent *(made his footstool*—an allusion again to Ps 110:1).

Second, his sacrifice was so efficacious that it guaranteed the final perfection of all those who were *being made holy.* This involved not only

of the Suffering Messiah found in Isaiah 50:5, "The Sovereign Lord has opened my ears, and I have not been rebellious; I have not drawn back," we see that the same concept is presented: the willingness of the Messiah to undergo the pain and suffering of the Cross. The ideas may be harmonized thus: "A body you have prepared for me which involves ears opened to your voice to do your will."

the regeneration of the spirit and the salvation of the soul, but also, the resurrection of the body of each true believer. The little-understood term *sanctified* of the KJV has been properly replaced in the NIV by the words *being made holy*. It is both an accomplished fact (10:10) and a continuing process (10:14), a phenomenon found frequently in Scripture. We may not understand such a mystery, but we can revel in its reality, as the writer intends us to do. All progress in the spiritual life comes from personally apprehending a fact that is already true. To put it simply, we must see what we already *are* by God's grace, in order to manifest that fact by godly behavior.

To show that such a condition completely fulfills the promises of the new covenant, the writer quotes again Jeremiah 31:33-34, introducing it with the words *The Holy Spirit also testifies . . .* This reveals once more his conviction that the prophets wrote by the inspiration and authority of God. Verse 16 highlights the new understanding of morality which regeneration gives (1 Jn 5:20); and verse 17 reminds us again of the wonder of total forgiveness of sins. This leads to the simple but conclusive statement of verse 18: where sins have been forgiven, no further sacrifice would do!

The Aaronic priesthood; the tabernacle with its typology, its cleansing rituals and animal sacrifices; and the dietary limitations of Israel—all found completion in the once-for-all sacrifice of Jesus and his Melchizedek priesthood. The new covenant is in force for all who truly believe. "The old has gone, the new has come!" (2 Cor 5:17).

The Privileges of Faith (10:19-25) The result of the operation of the new covenant in believers' lives is a highly visible transformation of their behavior. It flows from an inward change of attitude which is not dependent on outward circumstances. Believers become highly motivated to live at a new level of behavior and need only a bit of guidance about the *form* that new behavior should take. This powerful new motivation

---

10:20 The thought of Jesus' body as a curtain or veil brings to mind the words of Charles Wesley, "Veiled in flesh, the Godhead see, Hail th'incarnate Deity," and the statement of John 1:14, "The Word became flesh and made his dwelling [tabernacled] among us." It was the human body of Jesus which made it difficult for his disciples to believe that he was also God. It was like the curtain before the Holy of Hollies that hid God from the presence of

and its legitimate expressions now concern our author.

Twice in verses 19-31 the writer uses the phrase *we have*. Following these, there is thrice repeated the words *let us*. The *we haves* mark provision; *let us* indicates privilege.

First, *we have confidence to enter the Most Holy Place*. That "Most Holy Place" is the new life in the Spirit which the New Covenant provides ("I live in a high and holy place, but also with him who is contrite and lowly in spirit"—Is 57:15). As we have seen, it is that part of our humanity (the regenerated human spirit which puts us in touch with heaven) where God and humans meet. Through the death of Jesus a way has been opened for us so we may function as spiritual men and women. When Jesus' blood was shed on the cross, the veil before the Holy of Holies was supernaturally torn from top to bottom. That indicated that the way into the presence of God was now open to all who believe in Jesus. We can, therefore, enter with boldness and with no uncertainty as to our acceptance, since everything rests on the blood of Jesus. There is no doubt about our effectiveness, since we are now, to use Paul's helpful term, "colaborers with God." When we work, he will work too, and when we bear witness, he will speak through us.

It would be difficult to overestimate the value of confidence in human motivation. It is the proffered goal of any number of special courses, weekend retreats, training classes and personal development programs today. Confidence training is the cry of the hour. In the first century, too, men clearly understood that a confident spirit was essential to success in any enterprise. But as the psalmist made abundantly clear,

Unless the LORD builds the house,

its builders labor in vain.

Unless the LORD watches over the city,

the watchmen stand guard in vain. (Ps 127:1)

By itself, human effort is doomed to ultimate failure. Only that jointly shared effort, when God works through expectant humanity, can be

---

the priests in the Holy Place. But now that curtain/body no longer hides God from our eyes. The reference in Hebrews 10:20 undoubtedly recalls the statement in 6:19 that the Christian's hope of full acceptance before God is like an anchor for the soul; "it enters the inner sanctuary behind the curtain, where Jesus, who went before us, has entered on our behalf."

permanently successful. Confidence born of that conviction will always prevail.

But believers have more than a confident spirit. They are also reminded that (2) *we have a great priest over the house of God.* All that the writer has said about the Melchizedek priesthood of Jesus is recalled here. Believers have not only a confident spirit, but also a competent advocate. He is continually available, completely aware of our present situation, and vitally involved with us in working all things together for good. His great concern is the welfare of each member of the household of God, and "we are his house," as the writer has told us unmistakably in 3:6.

Encouraged by these two powerful resources, a confident spirit and a competent advocate, believers are now exhorted to three specific activities. (1) *Let us draw near to God with a sincere heart.* This "drawing near" must be the motive for all subsequent action. It includes more than formal prayer, since the present tense infers a continual drawing near. As the wick of a lamp continually draws oil for the light, so let us continually draw from God the strength and grace we need to function. This must be done (a) *sincerely,* without religious pretense; (b) *believingly,* in simple faith that God means what he says; (c) *without guilt,* having cleansed the conscience by reliance on the sprinkled blood of Jesus; and (d) *with integrity,* in line with our public profession of commitment to Christ expressed in our baptism. This continual drawing near to God is the great privilege of every believer in Jesus, in contrast to the remoteness of the old covenant which excluded everyone from the holy places except the priests. Even they could not enter except under the most stringent conditions. This "drawing near" is that "access by faith into this grace in which we now stand" which Paul describes in Romans 5:2.

Again the writer exhorts, (2) *Let us hold unswervingly to the hope we profess, for he who promised is faithful.* Here *profess* is seen as equivalent to "confess," for if we have drawn near to God, then surely the next logical step is to share the certainty of our hope with others. We can share our great expectation with confidence because *he who promised is faithful.* If those who hear us will act in faith as we have acted; they will experience the same blessing, for God is no respecter of persons. He will do as much for the man or woman next door as he has done for you; he will do as much for the janitor as he will do for the boss, and vice versa. We need not fear that God will let us down as his witnesses by showing favoritism to certain ones. He is faithful to keep his promise to anyone.

Another privilege believers may exercise is summarized in verse 24, (3) *Let us consider how we may spur one another on toward love and good deeds.* The supportive love of Christians for one another is a powerful factor in maintaining spiritual vigor. It needs to be awakened in both ourselves and others. That does not envision finger-shaking and lecturing, but encouraging words and good example.

Two suggestions are made to bring this about. First, *let us not give up meeting together, as some are in the habit of doing.* Corporate worship is not an option for a Christian; it is a necessity. It certainly includes regular attendance at church meetings, but means more than that. It means a willingness to help struggling faith whenever Christians meet. The author had already noted the bad effects of neglecting this on the part of some (3:13). Perhaps those who were hardened felt themselves to be sufficient in themselves, needing no one's help. One commentator suggests that if the real reasons for such separation were recorded, they might be easily recognizable in the modern church (Wiley 1959:342). If church services grow dull or boring they need renewal, not abandonment. The gathering of Christians should be an uplifting and exciting occasion. History has repeatedly shown that where this is neglected or permitted to dim, dullness and blandness soon follow.

A second suggestion for spurring one another on is also given: *Let us encourage one another—and all the more as you see the Day approaching.* The destruction of the temple and of the city of Jerusalem was just around the corner. The empire seethed with unrest and premonitions of disaster. These frightening omens were not viewed as signs of God's inability to control his world, as many interpret similar events today. Rather, they were indications that God was working out his predicted purposes just as Jesus, the prophets and the apostles had foretold. No one could know the hour when "the Day" would begin, but its coming was certain and apparently imminent to them. The Lord himself had instructed his disciples: "When these things begin to take place, stand up and lift up your heads, because your redemption is drawing near" (Lk 21:28).

It is now apparent as we look back over the centuries that it has been the will of God to have each generation feel that it is living in the very last days of civilization. Each century has found the church fearing the cataclysms of its own time as the last to come. Yet, inexorably, each passing century has moved the world nearer the final end. This sense of imminence is God's device to keep believers expectant and full of hope in the midst of the world's darkness. Evil becomes more subtle in our own day, and the difference between truth and error more difficult to detect. The raucous voices of the age pour forth deceitful lies and society becomes permeated with false concepts widely viewed as truth. We too need to gather together to encourage each other and renew our hope by sturdy reaffirmations of the eternal truths of God's Word.

We are a privileged people; privileged to draw near to the living God; privileged to speak out concerning our flaming hope; and privileged to stir one another up to love and good works. Carl F. H. Henry has well said, "Many Christians now live among neighbors who, swept by tides of immorality, fear herpes more than they fear Hades, and some even think God is a lofty synonym for gobbledygook" (Henry 1989: 152). Every age of Christians has had to live in such a world, and today's Christians are no exception. They must take care, therefore, that their Christian witness is real, practically expressed and based on a thorough knowledge of who they are in Christ. Let no one take this lightly, for in the next section our author flashes a brilliant red light of warning.

A Fourth Warning Against Apostasy (10:26-31) The writer includes himself ("we") as needing this warning also for it encompasses those who have received a full knowledge *(epignōsis)* of the truth. It is directed to those who *deliberately keep on sinning* after they fully understand the way of escape in Jesus. It adds seriousness to the exhortation of verse

---

10:25 Of *the Day* Hughes properly says: "When spoken of in this absolute manner, 'the Day' can mean only the last day, that ultimate eschatological day, which is the day of reckoning and judgment, known as the Day of the Lord" (1977:416). This, however, does not envision a 24-hour period, but a longer, indefinite time, when all the events foretold by the prophets will be fulfilled. It would begin with the Second Coming of Jesus (9:28) and would extend through the judgments at the beginning and end of the millennium (Rev 20), to the creation of the new heavens and earth.

25 not to abandon meeting together with other Christians (as the initial Greek *gar,* "for," indicates). This recalls John's warning in 1 John 2:19 concerning those who "went out from us." "Their going," he says, "showed that none of them belonged to us." They had known the way of life, but had not chosen to avail themselves of it, and one early sign of heart apostasy is an unwillingness to continue association with true believers.

Yet despite the advantage of full enlightenment, if there is no change in behavior and sin continues to dominate the life of professed believers, they will find no other hiding place from God's wrath, for there is no other sacrifice than Christ's which will avail for sin. Since by unchanged behavior such individuals give evidence that Christ's sacrifice is rejected, the one way of escape is rejected also. Only judgment and "blazing fire" after death awaits, as one of the enemies of God (2 Thess 1:7). This behavior parallels those "having fallen away" of 6:6, where apostasy also led to irremediable judgment.

The NIV has properly translated the opening phrase of verse 26 as, *if we deliberately keep on sinning.* It is not a sin one can stumble into suddenly. It is not the normal falterings of a Christian still learning how to walk in the Spirit. It has been well termed "the leukemia of noncommitment." It is choosing to live for self behind a Christian veneer and refusing to be delivered from sin's reign by the past sacrifice and present high priestly ministry of Jesus. It is not continual sinning from ignorance as many church members manifest, but occurs after full enlightenment. Such people know of the power of Christ to deliver, but have not chosen to avail themselves of it. Their life may appear to be fairly respectable when judged by the world's standards, but what it is like in God's eyes is described in verses 28-30.

The argument proceeds from the less to the greater, very much as the

---

10:26 Bruce remarks, "We shall not properly understand the anxiety [in the early church] which this problem caused unless we realize that the kind of sin which in practice aroused greatest concern was sexual irregularity. It was precisely here that the ordinary canons of everyday behavior differed most as between Christians and pagans. We may think today that equal attention ought to be paid to the other six deadly sins; the fact remains that this was the one which involved the greatest heart-searching in the Christian community" (1964:260). A refusal to follow Christian standards of morality may well mark the beginnings of the kind of apostasy brought before us in 10:26-31.

writer had done in 2:2-3. If immediate death was the penalty for violating the law of Moses (which was but a shadow or picture), how much more should one expect severe judgment for continually rejecting, knowingly and deliberately, the reality which is Jesus and his sacrifice! What they have done is threefold:

1. They have *trampled the Son of God under foot!* The writer chooses a title for Jesus which emphasizes his right to be Lord over all. To trample him under foot is to spurn his right to govern life. Lip service is paid to Christian truth but life is lived as one pleases, even adopting the world's values and standards. As one poet has described it:

He lived for himself, and himself alone;

For himself, and none beside.

Just as if Jesus had never lived,

And as if he had never died!

2. They have treated as something common or trivial the blood of the covenant which has power to make one holy. They have regarded the blood of Jesus as having no more value than the blood of any other man, and therefore, in practice, insisted that religious activities ought to be enough to satisfy God. And they are saying this even though they have previously acknowledged that the death of Christ has ruled out such means. Once they regarded themselves as holy (sanctified) by the blood of Jesus, but now they deny this and reject the cross as unnecessary for acceptance before God.

3. They insult the Spirit of grace. The full understanding of redemptive truth, the awareness that the blood of Jesus can make one holy, the pleasures of meeting together with other Christians; all have been a gracious ministry of the Holy Spirit to the individuals considered here. Now these are being rejected and treated with contempt. It is an egregious insult to the One who was sent to draw men and women to salvation. It actually means to become guilty of the sin which Jesus called "an eternal sin," unpardonable in any age (Mk 3:29).

Verse 30 supports this view of coming judgment with two references to the Song of Moses, found in Deuteronomy 32. The first refers to the destruction of apostates and is quoted also by Paul in Romans 12:20 in a possibly similar connection. The second quote, however, looks more to the severity of God on those of his own who presumptuously play with sin even when knowing better. Such a case is that of David in 2 Samuel 24, who is given a choice of three painful penalties because of his sin in numbering the people of Israel against the express prohibition of the Lord. If even a greatly beloved believer like David could be dealt with severely by God, how much more would the apostate feel the full extent of divine wrath!

In either case, says our author in verse 31, *It is a dreadful thing to fall into the hands of the living God.* To encounter the living God in the full majesty of his holiness is a terrifying and awesome experience. In the first case cited, it is to experience after death the eternal judgment of raging fire "that will consume the enemies of God." The second case is to know in this life the heavy hand of God's displeasure because of deliberate and sinful choices which one is reluctant to give up. Only God can tell the difference between these two cases, for in human eyes they may appear indistinguishable. But that is the purpose for such warnings as we find in Hebrews. As the writer has said: "See to it, brothers, that none of you has a sinful, unbelieving heart" (3:12), "Let us, therefore, be careful that none of you be found to have fallen short" (4:1), and "Let us make every effort to enter that rest, so that no one will fall" (4:11). God is not a power to trifle with, for he can do what we cannot do, namely, read hearts. He can be ruthless if it is necessary to waken those sinners to the evil results they are embracing. That ruthlessness is a hidden blessing when the heart is unaware that it is ignoring the death of Jesus as the only adequate sacrifice for sin. Behind his severity is mercy toward those destroying themselves in unbelief. God lovingly seeks to waken them to what they are doing before they reach that stage of heart-hardening which deliberately rejects Christ. Beyond that point lies the unpardonable sin.

Encouragement to Persevere (10:32-39) Once again, as in chapter 6, we see the writer's confidence that most of those he addresses are not apostate, as he describes in verses 32-34. He seeks to recall them to the love and steadfastness they had exhibited when their faith in Jesus was new. They had *received the light* as had also those now threatening apostasy, as verse 26 makes clear. But most had: (1) accepted *insult and persecution* to their own person, or supported others so treated; (2)

visited and sustained those put in prison for their faith; and (3) actually felt joy over watching their property confiscated, since they took comfort in the fact that their true treasures were in heaven, not on earth.

Such actions were the product of true faith, and he urges them to keep this confident faith in verses 35-36, since perseverance is the proof of reality. The persecutions and injustices they endured presented strong temptations to give up, to accept the values of society around, and to forget what they had learned about the realities of life, death and eternity. Many are tempted today to *throw away [their] confidence.* Confidence is what motivates appropriate action in view of the times in which one lives.

Carl Henry captures the possibilities of the hour in which we now live: "All the modern gods are sick and dying. The nations that long lusted after power are now terrified by it. Sex has played itself out for many who thought an infinity of it would be heaven on earth. The almighty dollar is falling like a burned-out star. It is a day made-to-order for sons of the prophets, for sons of the apostles, for Protestant Reformers, and for evangelical giants" (Henry 1986:107).

Times of danger especially call for renewed confidence, for confidence in Christ anchors the soul in times of pressure. To throw it away through doubt or neglect is to miss the incredibly rich reward that is waiting just around the corner. The coming of Christ is what God has promised (Acts 3:19-20) and for which faith waits (1 Thess 1:10). *You need to persevere,* says the writer. Patience is a moment-by-moment quality, one which grows with practice. As the writer has already said,

---

10:37-38 The Hebrew of the Habakkuk quotation reads:
For the revelation awaits an appointed time;
   it speaks of the end and will not prove false.
Though it linger, wait for it;
   it will certainly come and will not delay.
See, he is puffed up;
   his desires are not upright—
   but the righteous will live by his faith. (Hab 2:3-4)
The Septuagint text reads:
   Because the vision is yet for an appointed time,
   and it will appear at length and not in vain;
   if he is late, wait for him;
   because he will surely come, he will not delay.
   If he draws back, my soul has no pleasure in him,
   but my righteous one will live by faith [faithfulness].

it is "through faith and patience" that we inherit what has been promised (6:12).

The quotation from Habakkuk 2:3-4 which appears in verses 37-38 is taken from the Septuagint version. The author has made certain changes which adapt it to his specific purposes, without changing its basic thrust. Habakkuk speaks of a revelation which is coming; Hebrews changes it to a person. Since Jesus is both a person and God's last word to man (1:1), the change is appropriate. The main thrust of the quotation is for those who are made righteous by God. Faith will be the center around which all of life revolves. To shrink back from that is to reveal oneself as yet unrighteous and therefore not pleasing to God.

The writer introduces this quotation with the words *For in just a very little while.* These words serve to underscore the emphasis in Scripture on prophetic fulfillment. It has been characteristic of days of decline in the church to lose sight of the hope of Christ's coming. Such weakening of hope invariably gives rise to programs for world betterment which lead Christians to forsake the biblical methods of God's working in society and to become involved in efforts to improve the world without the message of the cross of Christ. These causes become especially appealing when the passage of centuries dims the hope of the Second Coming. Scoffers arise, as Peter predicted, who would say, "Where is this 'coming' he promised? Ever since our fathers died, everything goes on as it has since the beginning of creation" (2 Pet 3:3-4).

How can we align *in just a very little while* with 2,000 years of waiting?

It is clear that the writer of Hebrews feels free to rearrange the order of the sentences here and to put a somewhat different emphasis on the words. The revelation (or vision) which is to come, seen in the Hebrew text, is viewed by the writer as a reference to Christ. He denotes him as "the Coming One," which is the title given to the Messiah by John the Baptist (Mt 11:3). When the Hebrew text says, "Behold his soul is puffed up . . . but the righteous shall live by faith," it is a test to distinguish the coming prophet from one who is false. The LXX says instead, "If he draws back, . . ." which seems to be the result that follows one whose "desires are not right." The writer of Hebrews adopts that wording but refers it to the apostate who turns away from truth. By placing the phrase "my righteous one" before this, he makes it the subject of both parts of the verse. His thought is, if the righteous one endures by faith, he will gain the promised reward; if he draws back, he will show himself apostate. This freedom to rearrange an Old Testament text without destroying its basic meaning is characteristic of the New Testament writers who knew themselves to be the spokespersons of the Holy Spirit.

Peter helps, of course, with his reminder that "with the Lord a day is like a thousand years, and a thousand years are like a day." By that reckoning it has only been two days since Jesus left us with a promise to return. Further, as we have seen, it is a great mistake to project the limitations of time into eternity. These are two quite different things. Heaven, with all its implications of "absent from the body, present with the Lord" is fully experienced at the death of a believer, and thus the coming of the Lord is never any further away than one's personal death. We need to bear in mind our Lord's words to the persecuted church of Smyrna: "Be faithful, even to the point of death, and I will give you the crown of life" (Rev 2:10).

In verse 39, the writer places himself in the picture again, but this time identified clearly with *those who believe and are saved.* The two groups he addresses throughout the letter are here placed in direct contrast. Some are "shrinking back" and are headed for destruction. Others, the majority he feels, continue to believe and thus experience the saving of their souls. This is exactly what Jesus had promised to persecuted saints in Luke 21:19: "By standing firm, you will gain life."

This reference in Habakkuk to the faith by which the righteous shall live serves to introduce the last section of Hebrews with its brilliant focus on this operative word of the Christian life. Faith is the way we begin the life in Christ; faith is also the way it is maintained; and faith is what will bring us at last in triumph through the gates of glory into the very presence of the Lord himself. Chapters 11-13 provide a fitting climax to the letter, pursuing its themes with vivid pictures of faith in human lives.

□ Faith Made Visible (11:1-40)

Who are the heroes and heroines of the twentieth century? Human nature continually seeks a model to follow. Remember Elvis Presley in the pop musical world, followed by the Beatles and so many others? In the realm of science, there was Albert Einstein; in statesmanship, Winston

Notes: **11:1** Scholars debate the exact meaning of the words *hypostasis* ("assurance" or "substance") and *elenkos* ("certainty" or "evidence"). The NIV and RSV follow the first set of meanings ("assurance" and "certainty"); the KJV, the latter. Westcott points out that the KJV text reflects the unanimous usage of the Greek and Latin fathers, and, I believe, is more in line with the argument of Hebrews to this point. To say, "Faith is the substance of things

Churchill; in social work, Mother Teresa. One thoughtful contemporary, George F. Will, has chosen five men who were models for the last millennium (since 1000 A.D.): Machiavelli, Luther, Washington, Jefferson and Lincoln. In the religious honor roll of this century, surely the name of Billy Graham would appear, along with Aleksandr Solzhenitsyn, Martin Luther King, Jr., and of course, Mother Teresa. None of these names was known to the first-century world, yet the names of heroes and heroines of that time, recorded in the eleventh chapter of Hebrews, are still known around the world as models of faith and courage. We are invited now to consider the contribution each has made to our lives today.

The Nature of Faith (11:1-3) Hebrews 11 has been called the great faith chapter. What, exactly, is faith? If it is so important to the redemptive process, we must have a clear understanding of its nature. That need is supplied in verses 1-2. Faith, according to the NIV text, is always two things: (1) a sense of assurance within us *(being sure of what we hope for)* and (2) a certainty that there are realities which we cannot see with our physical eyes *(certain of what we do not see)*. A slightly different sense is conveyed by the KJV text, which I prefer at this point. Paul, in Colossians 1:5, sees faith and love as flowing out of the hope awakened by the gospel. Hope, which "springs eternal in the human breast," comes first. Then, faith sees freedom from sin on the basis of Christ's sacrifice, a consequent loving relationship to God, peace with one's neighbors and joy in the midst of life (all *what we hope for*). These realities, though invisible, are personally appropriated; as a result, love for both God and others flows from the sense of gratitude which faith has awakened. Thus, the famous triumvirate of "faith, hope, and love" are central to all Christian living.

This quality of faith is *what the ancients were commended for.* This is the theme of the rest of the chapter, consisting of a list of those who triumphed in God's eyes because of their faith. Verse 3 provides an example of faith's ability to see invisible realities. No one can see the

---

hoped for" is to see faith as being able to enjoy *in the present* something intended largely for the future. This is surely the sense intended in 6:5, "tasted . . . the powers of the coming age." Thus the invisible entities such as love, peace, joy, courage are made evident in the lives of those who walk by faith. Hence my title for this chapter—"Faith Made Visible."

words by which God brought the universe into being, but since that is the statement of Scripture (Genesis 1 records 9 times "God said"), faith understands that behind everything visible is the invisible command of God. The statement *what is seen was not made out of what was visible* constitutes a scientific truth which modern physicists recognize: behind everything visible is invisible energy. Faith in God's revelation is a way of grasping reality, without necessarily comprehending all the steps that may be involved.

Verses 4-38 list examples of this kind of faith in men and women of the biblical past. The American philosopher Henry David Thoreau is famous for the remark, "If a man does not keep pace with his companions, perhaps it is because he hears a different drummer." That is a good description of the men and women listed here. They hear another drumbeat which others do not, and this accounts for the way they often act contrary to normal expectations. The first three examples, Abel, Enoch and Noah, show us the nature of faith. The rest show how faith behaves in real life.

The Qualities of Faith (11:4-7) Though the writer has, throughout the epistle, held up Abraham as our model of faith and perseverance, verses 4-7 indicate that true faith was practiced from the very beginning, even before the Flood. As in a modern docudrama, Abel appears first to testify to the value of faith. He and his older brother Cain lived when the world was young. They enjoyed what we would call today "the simple life," which clearly included a recognition of God and a need for a personal relationship. Each brought an offering which reflected his occupation: Cain, the farmer, brought fruits and grains; Abel, the shepherd, brought fat from the firstborn of his flock.

It is a mistake to read into this Genesis account any hidden reasons for God's acceptance of Abel's offering and rejection of Cain's. Various explanations have been offered, but the writer is silent about everything

---

11:4 The LXX says Cain's offering was not "divided rightly" though it offers no explanation as to what that meant. Philo described Abel's offering as "living" in contrast to Cain's which was "lifeless." Josephus suggested that God is more pleased with things which grow spontaneously than with that which is "forcibly produced by the ingenuity of covetous man," by which he apparently meant that Cain had to work harder than Abel! The Puritan scholar John Owen, followed by many today, linked the offerings with Hebrews 9:22, "without the shedding of blood there is no forgiveness" and insisted that Cain's bloodless offering was

except that God "spoke well" of Abel's offering because it was "better" than Cain's. The word "better" is *pleiona,* which means "greater" or "more important" as suggested by its use in Luke 12:23: "Life is *more than* food, and the body *more than* clothes." If Abel's sacrifice was more important than Cain's, what made it so? The reason suggested is that it came from a heart made righteous by faith! If Abraham's faith was "credited to him as righteousness" (Rom 4:9), so also was Abel's. Bruce comments on this, "Sacrifice is acceptable to God not for its material content, but in so far as it is the outward expression of a devoted and obedient heart" (1964:283).

We are not told just how God made known to the two brothers his acceptance of one and rejection of the other. Genesis 4:7 indicates that when Cain learned that his offering was unacceptable, he grew angry and rebellious. This revealed the attitude of his heart toward the sovereign choices of God. Cain's subsequent murder of his brother showed his stubborn rejection of the opportunity God gave him to repent and to offer again, presumably with a contrite spirit. Cain's offering was rejected because a heart of pride and self-sufficiency lay behind it. This explanation fits well with the context of Hebrews where the writer repeatedly warns against possessing "an evil heart of unbelief."

The focus in 11:4, however, is not on Cain but on Abel. *By faith he still speaks,* says the author, *even though he is dead.* This is a direct allusion to Genesis 4:10, "Your brother's blood cries out to me from the ground." It must be linked also with Hebrews 12:24, where our author states that the blood of Jesus "speaks a better word than the blood of Abel." It is often suggested that the blood of Abel cries out for the final vindication promised to all the saints (2 Thess 1:6-7), but the blood of Jesus speaks of proffered forgiveness. This seems a likely explanation of the continuing testimony of Abel. His faith in God was one of trust and loving acceptance of whatever God sent. He was willing to wait for

---

the reason for his rejection. But neither offering is ever said to be a sin offering. The offering of firstfruits was included later under the law as acceptable worship of God. Scripture attaches no blame to Cain for the offering he brought; it was the condition of his heart in bringing it that caused its rejection.

11:5 Bruce (1964:286-289) gives excerpts from intertestamental wisdom literature which show how widely Enoch was accepted as the earliest of the prophets.

ultimate vindication of injustice and mistreatment. His faith teaches us that we must often wait for God's redress of injustice. We do so because we know God cannot ultimately fail to act.

Enoch, the seventh from Adam, appears next on the stage of testimony in verses 5-6. Two important things mark the character of Enoch's faith: (1) he pleased God by turning away from the godlessness of the world in which he lived and (2) he maintained a daily walk with God which grew so intimate that he was taken to heaven without experiencing death. The Genesis account (5:21-24) indicates that for the first 65 years of his life, Enoch did not walk with God. Presumably he went along with the deteriorating morality of his times, which Genesis 6:5 describes as, "The LORD saw how great man's wickedness on the earth had become, and that every inclination of the thoughts of his heart was only evil all the time." As Genesis 5:25 suggests, the event which changed Enoch's outlook was the birth of a son, whom he named Methuselah. Some scholars derive the meaning of Methuselah from the Hebrew root *muth,* which means "death," and translate the name "His death shall bring (it)." This would imply a revelation to Enoch of the coming judgment of the world by means of the Flood. The chronology of Genesis 5 places the Flood as occurring the year Methuselah died. In the New Testament, Jude 14-15 mentions such a prophecy given to Enoch, and much of the Wisdom literature of the intertestamental period views Enoch as a far-sighted prophet. At any rate, the Genesis account states that from the birth of Methuselah throughout the following 300 years, Enoch "walked with God." This turn in his life was a result of faith, and since faith always requires a word from God to rest upon, it confirms the idea that Enoch was given a revelation of a coming judgment which changed his life.

The walk with God which Enoch experienced was one of deepening intimacy. A walk implies a journey in a certain direction and at a measured and regular pace. Enoch's faith flourished as he walked and God bore witness to him that his daily life was pleasing in his eyes. Enoch is an example to the readers of Hebrews of what the writer longed to see happen to them: a steady, daily growth in grace achieved by the inner resources which God supplies to those who take him at his word and act in faith on what he has said. Enoch enjoyed the continuous presence of an unseen Person, and related his life daily to that Person. The result was a fellowship which death could not interrupt. He was translated to glory and was "not found," implying that someone searched for him for some time, but in vain. He and, later, Elijah are the only two individuals in the Scriptures who never died a physical death. They serve as precursors for a whole generation of Christians who will be so translated at the *parousia* of Jesus (1 Thess 4:17). We learn from Enoch that faith can draw inner strength from God to such a degree that it triumphs over the ravages of death.

Our author views Enoch's faith as so outstanding that it constitutes a general example for all time of how to come to God and to live pleasing to him. *Without faith it is impossible to please God,* he proclaims in verse 6. This brings to mind Paul's similar assertion, "the world through its wisdom did not know him" (1 Cor 1:21). It is impossible through human reasoning or scientific searching to find God: faith in God's self-revelation is essential! But that revelation is not confined to Scripture; it begins with nature as Paul forcefully states in Romans 1:19-20 and the psalmist declares in Psalms 8 and 19.

Hebrews 11:6 is a helpful answer to the persistent question: "What about the primitive peoples of the world who never hear the gospel?" This verse says: *anyone who comes to him [God] must believe that he exists and that he rewards those who earnestly seek him.* Nature presents overwhelming evidence of the existence of God. Elizabeth Barrett Browning has put its witness well:

Earth's crammed with heaven,

And every common bush aflame with God.

But only those who see take off their shoes,

The rest sit round it and pluck blackberries!

Only a deliberately resistant mind can set aside nature's testimony to the wisdom and power of an Intelligent Being beyond us. If the witness of nature leads an individual to an honest search for the Creator, God promises to help and *reward those who earnestly seek him.* More and more knowledge will be granted which, if followed, will lead to Jesus. As Peter declared in Acts 4:12, "Salvation is found in no one else, for there is no other name under heaven given to men by which we must be saved." What the writer is implying, by linking verse 6 with the life of Enoch, is that Enoch, seeking God and believing the word he was given, found

Christ by faith! So we learn from him that faith means turning from human wisdom to God's revelation and walking in daily obedience to it until it leads to a fellowship which death cannot interrupt!

The spotlight of witness then shifts to Noah, who illustrates for us a still different quality of true faith. His faith, too, saw what was invisible, namely the coming of the Flood! (vs. 7). He "saw" it because he believed the warning he received from God 120 years before the Flood came (Gen 6:3, 7). Moved by fear of that catastrophe, Noah obeyed God and built an ark of wood, by means of which his whole family was saved. Such obedient faith, the writer states, *condemned the world,* by showing how wrong it was. This made Noah an *heir of the righteousness that comes by faith.* In the phrase *condemned the world,* we may rightly visualize the mockery and jeering which Noah must have daily faced as he built a huge ship. He was a hundred miles from the nearest ocean, with a ship many times too big for his own needs, and when he had finished, he filled it with animals! Had he lived in our day he would have been dubbed, "Nutty Noah"! Yet Jesus used "the days of Noah" as representative of the condition of the world before his own return, and indicated that his followers must be prepared to face the same kind of scornful hostility that Noah met day after day.

Noah's faith persisted despite massive resistance, and that can only occur when there is an inward change of spirit that is caused by the presence of God. That is what is meant by Noah becoming *heir of the righteousness that comes by faith.* His faith, like Abraham's, was "credited to him for righteousness." He is, in fact, the first individual to be called righteous in the Scriptures (Gen 6:9). His sturdy, obedient faith stands forever as an example of persistence against hostility that marks those who are born of God and who cannot ever be lost. In these three men, Abel, Enoch and Noah, we are shown that faith waits, faith grows in intimacy, and faith persists. Without these qualities it is impossible to please God.

11:10 *A city which has foundations* . . . Nowhere in the Old Testament is there any mention of such a city. However, the concept of a city is prominent in the Old Testament from the beginning. Cain built a city in the land of Nod, naming it after his son Enoch (Gen 4:17), and after the flood men built the city of Babel, which they saw as an instrument to achieve fame and security (Gen 11:4). Abraham is called to leave the city of Ur of the Chaldees, a highly developed commercial center with schools and a library, and it should not be surprising that he would expect a city to be built ultimately in the land of Canaan

The Activities of Faith (11:8-38) "Faith without deeds is useless," says James (2:20). If there is true faith, there will be consequent actions. The writer now launches on a lengthy section in which he shows the variety of actions that can accompany faith, depending on the circumstances which an individual faces. The one mark that is shared by all these activities is that each is unusual—it is not the normal reaction ordinarily expected of those who face such situations. Faith makes some people act differently than others. They will not fit the common mold or drift along with the multitude.

The Faith of Abraham and Sarah (11:8-19) Already in Hebrews, Abraham has shared with Moses a prominent part as an example of faith in the redemptive process. Again, he appears as the pre-eminent role model for all believers in Christ. Verses 8-19 are devoted almost exclusively to Abraham's faith and the author's comments on it. He singles out the highlights of Abraham's life, beginning with his call to leave Mesopotamia and culminating with his willingness to sacrifice Isaac at God's command. At every point, Abraham responded to a promise of God with unwavering obedience. That is the writer's chief point. God promised Abraham a land, a posterity, a great name and universal influence (Gen 12:1-3). Abraham believed God and left his kinfolk, his present comforts and prospects, and, at the age of seventy-five, set out for Canaan, a land he had never visited and knew nothing about (v. 8). When he got there he lived as a resident alien, residing in tents and owning nothing except the cave of Machpelah in Hebron, where he buried his wife, Sarah. The motive for this remarkable behavior was his anticipation that God would fulfill his promise and produce on earth, *a city with foundations, whose architect and builder is God* (vv. 9-10). It is amazing how far Abraham saw by faith. He lived two thousand years before Christ, and we live two thousand years after him. Yet Abraham, believing that what God had said would take place, looked across forty centuries of time and beyond to

to which he was called. This would be what Paul calls "the present city of Jerusalem" which pictures the "Jerusalem that is above" which he says is "our mother" (Gal 4:26). Just as the land of Canaan itself was a picture of a heavenly rest, so other earthly cities could only faintly shadow the city with foundations which God would plan and build. It would be this heavenly city which Abraham's faith envisaged that would enable him to wait patiently through a lifetime of nomadic existence.

the day when God would bring to earth a city with eternal foundations. Abraham saw what John saw in Revelation: a city coming down from heaven onto earth (Rev 21). That is what Abraham longed for; an earth run after God's order, where people would dwell together in peace, harmony, blessing, beauty and liberty. Because of that hope he was content to dwell his whole life in tents, looking for God's fulfillment. Abraham shows us that faith seizes upon a revealed event and lives in anticipation of it. Faith gives purpose and destination to life. The hope of achieving a utopian city of peace and universal blessing is what we hold out for even today; "Thy kingdom come, thy will be done on earth as it is in heaven."

The second highlight of Abraham's faith centered on God's promise of a posterity (vv. 11-12). This involved Sarah as well, for though Abraham was now a hundred years old, and Sarah ninety, God had expressly told Abraham that he would have a son who would produce a long line of descendants. Paul, in Romans 4:19, observes: "Without weakening in his faith, he faced the fact that his body was as good as dead . . . and that Sarah's womb was also dead. Yet he did not waver through unbelief regarding the promise of God."

We must not exclude Sarah from this reckoning of those who triumphed by faith, as the NIV rendering of verse 11 does. For though she laughed incredulously when she overheard God's promise to Abraham that she would bear a son (Gen 18:11-12), nevertheless, God countered her incredulity with the question, "Is anything too hard for the LORD?" Those challenging words would surely have been the source of her meditation in the days that followed. Genesis 21:1 states, "Now the LORD was gracious to Sarah as he had said, and the LORD did for Sarah what he had promised." God's invariable method for fulfilling a promise is to awaken faith first in the recipient. Sarah's growth in grace and spiritual maturity is recognized in 1 Peter 3:6, and all this would powerfully

11:11 Many commentators are troubled by the phrase which the NIV translates *was enabled to become a father,* especially since in the Greek "Sarah herself" is in the nominative case which would make her the subject of the sentence. The Greek is *dynamin eis katabolēn spermatos elaben,* literally, "received power unto the laying-down of seed." It is generally agreed that this refers to the depositing of semen by the male, rather than the presenting of an ovum by the female. Thus Abraham must be the subject here. Two alternatives have been proposed for understanding the phrase *autē Sarra steira* ("Sarah herself

support the design of our author by including Sarah's name deliberately. She shared with Abraham that faith which produced *descendants as numerous as the stars in the sky and as countless as the sand on the seashore.*

It is highly unlikely, given our author's precise use of language, that these two phrases should both describe the same descendants of Abraham, whether they are physical or spiritual. Abraham was first promised seed "like the dust of the earth" (Gen 13:16). Then some thirteen years later, when God announced the birth of Isaac within a year, Abraham was shown the stars and the promise was given, "Look up at the heavens and count the stars—if indeed you can count them. . . . So shall your offspring be" (Gen 15:5). This widely separated revelation suggests the phrases should be understood as a reference to two lines of posterity: a heavenly seed *(as numerous as the stars in the sky)* which would embrace all who fit Paul's description: "If you belong to Christ, then you are Abraham's seed, and heirs according to the promise" (Gal 3:29); and an earthly line *(as countless as the sand on the seashore),* which includes all the physical descendants of the twelve sons of Jacob. This would agree with Paul's statements in Romans 11:11-12 that despite the formation of the church (the heavenly seed), God has not yet finished with his people Israel (the earthly seed). As the writer of Hebrews has intimated, the time will come when God will fulfill the new covenant of grace to "the house of Israel and the house of Jacob." The blending of these two lines will be found in the city for which Abraham looked, on whose gates is written the names of the twelve tribes of Israel and on its foundations the names of the twelve apostles of the Lamb (Rev 21:12-14).

The writer comments, in verses 13-16, on these Old Testament names. They all died, he admits, without receiving the things promised, though they still expected God to fulfill his word to them. The fact that *they only saw them and welcomed them from a distance* indicates their under-

---

barren"). One is that taken by the NIV here; namely, that the phrase is a Hebraic circumstantial clause—"and Sarah herself was barren." The other possibility is that the phrase is a dative of accompaniment (with the iota subscripts absent in the uncial script). Thus we should translate: "By faith he [Abraham] also, together with Sarah, received power to beget a child . . ." (Bruce 1964:302—see the discussion 299-302.) In either case, the explicit mention of Sarah should be seen as a commendation of her faith as well.

standing that the promises were in the future and would have spiritual as well as physical fulfillment. For this reason, their own imminent deaths did not diminish their confidence that the promises would be fulfilled. This lively faith was shown by their willingness to abide as aliens and strangers in the land they had been promised. Toward the end of his life, Abraham described himself as such in Genesis 23:4. Though he and his son and grandsons could have returned to Mesopotamia had they so chosen, as Jacob did for a while, yet their faith in the promise of their own land not only kept them in Canaan, but also led them to understand that eventually they would live in that city of God which would come down from heaven. Because their faith grew to encompass eternal realities as well as earthly prospects, the writer declares that *God is not ashamed to be called their God.* Once again we see the deliberate link between the visible and the invisible. The land of Canaan was a picture of the heavenly country which would be theirs by faith, as 4:8-9 asserts. Since, as we have seen, "faith is being sure of what we hope for," this meant that they were already enjoying, in their inner lives, the intimate blessings that the resurrected body promised when the city of God came down from heaven (Rev 21:10). Such inner fulfillment is the gift of faith to those who today are willing to look beyond death to God's day of perfect fulfillment. We cannot demand instant answers from God for all our earthly problems, but we can *welcome them from a distance.* We must not lose faith that God will satisfy every promise.

Having expanded our understanding of the faith of the patriarchs, our author returns to the severest test of Abraham's faith, and its most glorious triumph, the sacrifice of Isaac (vv. 17-19). Emphasis is laid on the fact that Abraham was asked to slay his son Isaac, even though he had received promises that Isaac would establish the guaranteed posterity. Ishmael was also a son of Abraham, but only Isaac was the son of promise. That is the meaning of *one and only son.* Some have criticized God for subjecting Abraham to such unbearable anguish, but it must be remembered that Abraham's faith in the loving character of God enabled him to solve this crisis. He reasoned that God was in full control of both death and life; he could restore as well as take. On that basis Abraham was able to carry through what was seen as a grisly task. Little of this is seen in the Genesis account (22:1-10), though Abraham did assure his servants that both he and the lad would return from the mountain. The substitution of a ram for the son was intended to portray that later scene at Golgotha when the Son of God would willingly lay down his life. It is, perhaps, this very scene that Paul has in mind when he writes, "He who did not spare his own Son, but gave him up for us all—how will he not also, along with him, graciously give us all things?" The restoration of Isaac to his father's arms is called a parable (Gk *parabolē*) of resurrection by the writer. So Abraham's faith reached the highest pinnacle of faith: belief in a resurrection that would fulfill all the promises of God.

The Faith of Isaac, Jacob and Joseph (11:20-22) The thought of a faith still trusting in the very face of death leads the writer to focus on Abraham's descendants—Isaac, Jacob and Joseph. They see their own deaths and yet look beyond in unwavering faith (vv. 20-22). The point about all three is that they clearly saw aspects of the future because they exercised faith in what was invisible at the present. Isaac, though not given to dramatic demonstrations of faith, could still foretell the subsequent character of his twin sons' lives, Jacob and Esau, because he understood, by faith, how each would relate to the program of God (Gen 27:27-29, 30-40). Jacob, in his earlier years, often found it difficult to trust God explicitly. But with Joseph in Egypt, he too saw the true relationship of Joseph's sons Manasseh and Ephraim in God's purposes. He dared, by faith, to transfer the birthright from Manasseh, the firstborn, to Ephraim, the younger (Gen 48). He did this, worshiping all the while the God who had foreordained this in wisdom. And Joseph, whose life was filled with dramatic examples of the power of faith, did not let his impending death alter his certainty that God would fulfill his promises concerning Israel. He gave instructions that when Israel would leave Egypt (over two centuries later), they should carry his bones with them and bury them in the land of promise. This Moses did (Ex 13:19), and Joseph's tomb is still visible at Shechem, as Joshua 24:32 records. These men were not dreamers or merely wishful thinkers; they "saw" invisible realities, and adapted their own lives and that of their descendants accordingly.

The Faith of Moses and the Israelites (11:23-29) The spotlight of witness shifts again, this time to the towering figure of Moses, who stands next only to Abraham as the quintessential believer in the Old Testament. Verses 23-29 touch on five highlights from his life, beginning with the faith of his parents and ending with the Israelites' passage over the Red Sea. Two reasons are given for the faith of Moses' parents, shown in the hiding of their infant son among the reeds of the Nile. They saw he was *no ordinary child, and they were not afraid of the king's edict.* The adjective *asteion* translated here as "no ordinary" child, is defined by Thayer as the opposite of *agroikos* which means "rustic" (Kistemaker 1984:344). It implies not merely a handsome or beautiful child, but a gifted and unusually promising one. Josephus, in his *Antiquities,* suggests that Moses' parents received a revelation from God concerning their son's destiny. This would explain why their action was *by faith* and strong enough that they were unafraid of the king's cruel command to kill all male Israelite babies. Since Jochebed, Moses' mother, was employed by Pharaoh's daughter to become Moses' nurse and help raise him to adulthood, the writer includes Moses' parents (Amram and Jochebed) as the molders of the faith of Moses himself.

So powerful was their influence on Moses that when he was forty years of age (Acts 7:23), having been trained in the culture of Egypt and even regarded as an heir to the throne itself, he renounced his earthly privileges. He went on to identify himself with the people of Israel and resolutely refused the royal title *son of Pharaoh's daughter* (vv. 24-25). Stephen, in Acts 7:20-38, tells us that Moses "thought that his own people would realize that God was using him to rescue them, but they did not." This suggests that Moses had a clear understanding of his calling from God, and his faith motivated his renunciation of Egypt. It was costly because he gave up *the treasures of Egypt* to suffer *disgrace for the sake of Christ.* Such disgrace (or "reproach") carried with it the promise of infinite reward (eternal life) which made the things he renounced appear paltry indeed. Such a renunciation is like the choices many Christians make today who choose to be faithful to moral principles, rather than to abandon them for the prospect of advancement or wealth.

11:26 It is difficult to know what aspects of Christ Moses saw that so powerfully turned him from the transient treasures and pleasures of Egypt. The Hebrew word for *Christ* ("Anointed One") did not have the associations with the life of Jesus that the word *Christ* has for us today. Yet there was an unmistakable Presence which Moses and other Old

The third mark of Moses' faith was that *he left Egypt, not fearing the king's anger* and *he persevered because he saw him who is invisible* (v. 27). Admittedly, he fled to save his life, but as the writer of Hebrews points out, it was not because he feared the anger of the king. Rather, since he fled *by faith,* it was because he knew God would fulfill his promise to deliver Israel. Moses would await God's timing for that deliverance. So he *persevered* in Midian for forty years, with his faith continually being renewed because *he saw him who is invisible.* That long, discouraging wait was possible only because Moses saw the unseen; he reckoned upon invisible realities, and God surprised him one day with a remarkable experience with a bush that burned but was not consumed!

Another biblical example of this kind of patient faith is David, who, knowing he had been anointed as king of Israel, nevertheless patiently waited for God to remove Saul from the throne. Such patience, for those who wait for recognition today, is rewarded by *him who is invisible.* God times such events, lifting up one and putting down another, according to his sovereign purposes. Peter exhorts us, "Humble yourselves, therefore, under God's mighty hand, that he may lift you up in due time" (1 Pet 5:6).

Our author leaps over the story of Moses' return to Egypt, his confrontations with the new Pharaoh and the shattering series of plagues which Pharaoh's intransigence brought upon Egypt. This brings us to the final, fateful night, when Moses and Israel kept the first Passover (v. 28). It was a crucial experience both for Israel and the church, as both look back to it as the paradigm of redemption. Central was the sprinkling of the blood of a lamb over the doorpost of each Israelite household. The angel of death would not enter where he saw the sprinkled blood. Paul refers to this incident in 1 Corinthians 6:7-8. Moses believed implicitly that this protection would work, and so it proved. Even Pharaoh's firstborn son lay dead the next morning with thousands of others throughout Egypt. In Israel, not one firstborn son perished, exactly as Moses had predicted. This act of faith broke the back of Pharaoh's resistance, and the Egyptians

---

Testament characters sensed, which they associated with God, and which they valued in a personal and intimate way (Ex 33:14-15). Paul could say of the Israelites in the wilderness, "they drank from the spiritual rock that accompanied them, and that rock was Christ" (1 Cor 10:3).

begged the Israelites to leave, even heaping upon them jewels and treasures to speed the process.

But in verse 29, the writer recounts the faith Moses and Israel had to exercise when the Egyptians changed their minds and pursued Israel with an army of chariots and soldiers. The waters of the Sea of Reeds (Hebrew text) flowed before Israel, and the army of Egypt was closing in behind. What could Israel do? God said to Moses, "Tell the Israelites to move on. Raise your staff and stretch out your hand over the sea to divide the water." By faith Moses obeyed, and by faith the waters were driven back all night by a powerful east wind (Ex 14). Israel's faith was shown when they passed between the walls of water and arrived safely on the far shore. When the Egyptians tried the same thing, Moses stretched out his staff, the waters returned, and all the Egyptian soldiers were drowned. Faith dares to obey despite apparent obstacles and difficulties. It pays no attention to impossibilities when God has spoken.

Faith, mighty faith, the promise sees

And looks to God alone.

Laughs at impossibilities,

And cries, "It shall be done."

Many Christians today face similar circumstances where it looks as if there is no way out. But God does not send believers out into a sea of trouble to drown; his promise is to see them through to the other side. As 1 Corinthians 10:13 promises, "He will also provide a way out so that you can stand up under it."

Faith Exhibited at Jericho (11:30-31) No further examples of Israel's faith are described until forty years later, when Joshua leads them against the city of Jericho, the first major obstacle to the conquest of the land of promise. This silence is the writer's way of recalling what he has already mentioned in chapters 3 and 4: the unbelief which the Israelites showed throughout their wilderness journeys. Not one Israelite who was twenty years or older when they left Egypt would enter Canaan, except Joshua and Caleb. But just as the faith of Moses had inspired some degree of faith in Israel while they were in Egypt, the faith of Joshua stirred the Israelites to act in faith before the walls of Jericho. The ancient city was actually a large fortress, 600 meters in circumference (Kistemaker 1984:347). It contained an armed garrison, filled with experienced warriors. These must be defeated before the valleys of Canaan could be occupied. Following the unique orders given him by the angelic Commander of the Army of the Lord, Joshua set the people marching around the fortress, once a day for six days, and seven times the seventh day. When they gave a great shout on the seventh day, the walls "came atumblin' down." By an earthquake, you may ask? Yes, perhaps so, but an earthquake that came in God's precise time and at God's precise place. The incident highlights God's ways of deliverance as being varied and often bizarre in the eyes of many. He is infinitely diverse in his solutions, and we make a great mistake in trying to predict his actions.

Along with the story of Jericho's overthrow, we read the remarkable account of Rahab the harlot (v. 31). She had heard of Israel's conquests at the Red Sea and in the wilderness and expected them to assault Jericho many years before. She knew that their victories came from their faith in God, and she "received the spies with peace" (literally) when Joshua sent them to spy out the city. Her motive was not merely to save her life and that of her family; she was convinced, as she said, that "the LORD your God is God in heaven above and on the earth below." That faith was honored when the walls of the city collapsed and all within were killed except Rahab and her family. That her faith was genuine is confirmed by Matthew when he lists her as one of the ancestors of Jesus. She went on to marry Salmon and became the mother of Boaz, and thus the great-grandmother of David. Faith overcame a sinful life, delivered her from a pagan religion. She was granted a place of honor among the heroes and heroines of faith. The incident also illustrates the fact that "in Christ there is neither male nor female." Rahab was a woman in a man's world, but faith accepts no such distinctions.

A Summary of the Faithful (11:32-38) This survey of the faith of men and women in the past could have gone on to greater lengths, but the author feels that his epistle must not become burdensome to read. He refers to others in more general terms, mentioning only six more names. Their varied actions of faith are successful, whether in triumph or in suffering (vv. 32-38). The six names span the history of Israel from the days of the judges to the early monarchy. Included are Gideon, noted for his victory over Midian with a reduced army of only 300 men; Barak, who was encouraged by the prophetess Deborah and defeated the Canaanite army of Sisera; Samson, famous as the muscleman of Israel, fatally susceptible to the charms of young women, but nevertheless the instrument of God to deliver Israel from Philistine oppression; Jephthah, haunted by his rash vow concerning his daughter, but also conqueror of the Ammonites and punisher of the tribe of Ephraim; David, Israel's greatest king and the author of many psalms, "a man after God's own heart"; and, finally, Samuel, first of the prophets and last of the judges, who lived by faith from his boyhood to his final days. Others are simply listed as *the prophets*, which would surely include the great names of Elijah, Elisha, Amos, Hosea, Isaiah, Jeremiah, Daniel, Ezekiel and others.

The faith these men possessed led them to three kinds of action (vv. 33-34). Faith helped some to govern—*conquered kingdoms* (David over the Philistines), *administered justice* (Solomon—1 Kings 21:9) and *gained what was promised* (Josh 21:43). Faith helped others to triumph over fearful odds—*shut the mouths of lions* (Dan 6), *quenched the fury of the flames* (Dan 3:17), and *escaped the edge of the sword* (2 Kings 6:11-18). Still others were enabled by faith to be mighty in battle—*whose weakness was turned to strength; and who became powerful in battle and routed foreign armies* (1 Sam 14:14). These were all actual historic incidents, familiar to the readers of this letter from the Old Testament accounts.

But faith was not confined to men only. Women of faith were also greatly benefited, receiving dead loved ones back to life. Notable in the Old Testament were the widow of Zarephath, whose son Elijah restored, even though she was not of Israel (1 Kings 17:24); and the woman of Shunem who called Elisha to raise her dead son because she knew him to be a man of God (2 Kings 4:8-37). The readers of Hebrews could also think of the widow of Nain, whose son Jesus raised, and of Lazarus whom Jesus restored to his sisters, Mary and Martha, and perhaps also of the widows in Joppa who rejoiced when Dorcas was restored to them by Peter. These resuscitations were not mentioned to establish a norm, but to show what powers faith could release when God chose to act.

Nor was faith always a means to triumph and victory. Verses 35-38 record the other side of the picture. The incidents described here seem to be drawn mainly from the days of the Maccabean revolt and the cruelties of the Syrian king Antiochus Epiphanes in the early second century B.C. The word for *tortured* reveals the type of torment used: a wheel or rack upon which the victim was stretched and then beaten to death. The *better resurrection* they looked for was not a return to this life, but the resurrection to eternal life, which was promised to all who were faithful unto death. The jeers, flogging, chains and prisons of verse 36 were experienced in many places and times, even by some recipients of this letter, as 10:32-34 declares. Jeremiah may have been the reference to some who were stoned, for tradition says he so died at the hands of the Jews in Egypt. Isaiah was thought to be sawed in half during the reign of Manasseh, the wicked son of King Hezekiah. Many were reduced to poverty and had to dress themselves in animal skins (Elijah, Elisha and John the Baptist, for example), and wandered about in deserts and mountains, living in caves because they were unacceptable to society. But the writer notes that the world was not worthy of them. God's heroes and heroines are often unrecognized while they are alive. Like Jesus himself, they are "despised and rejected of men." But what does that matter when the final triumph sees them honored and acclaimed before the whole universe? As another ardent Christian, Jim Elliot, put it: "He is no fool who gives what he cannot keep, to gain what he cannot lose."

One cannot think on these verses today and not notice the contrast with the so-called health-and-wealth gospel. For the person of faith, material comforts mean less and spiritual values mean more. The question of Jesus comes to mind: "What good is it for a man to gain the whole world, yet forfeit his soul?" The people of God may often be poor and despised, but their faith opens to them riches of spirit which the world has never known.

Something Better for Us (11:39-40) The closing verses (39-40) bring us back to the opening statement of the chapter, that faith *is what the ancients were commended for.* Though all those referred to by name or described by action in this chapter received commendation from God even in this life, yet they did not receive the promised city "with foundations" which Abraham sought (vv. 10 & 16). The reference to *foundations* indicates something material and earthly, rather than purely spiritual. They looked for more than their own personal satisfaction, but still longed to see God's purposes fulfilled on earth. The *something better for* *us* denotes the reality we have found already in Christ, which the men and women of faith in the Old Testament would attain only after their earthly life ended. We are already recipients of the blessings of the new covenant. They would not fully know them till the resurrection. The New Jerusalem, come down from heaven to earth, in which God will dwell among us and by which all the supernal vision of the prophets will be fulfilled, blends the two peoples of God together. The hope of being *made perfect* includes the hope of physical resurrection, as many Scriptures declare. In that "first resurrection" (Rev 20:6-7) believers of both old and new covenants will join. This is the way that *together with us would they be made perfect.* This is the mystery of God's will which Paul describes in Ephesians 1:9-10 "to be put into effect when the times will have reached their fulfillment—to bring all things in heaven and on earth together under one head, even Christ."

What transcendent glory is described in those words, no one now really knows. John gives us the best description in Revelation 4—5. There the redeemed are gathered from all ages, amid millions of angels, to sing the praises of the One who redeemed them from the miseries and death which sin causes, and gave them an eternal ministry of glory and power beyond human description. The Redeemer will be forever the center of universal worship. It will be as Anne Cousin writes:

> The bride eyes not her garment,
> But her dear bridegroom's face;
> I will not gaze at glory,
> But on my King of grace:
> Not at the crown He giveth,
> But on his pierced hand;
> The Lamb is all the glory
> Of Emmanuel's land.
> ("The Sands of Time Are Sinking")

Calvin caught the thrust of this chapter and said, "If those on whom the great light of grace had not yet shone showed such surpassing constancy in bearing their ills, what effect ought the full glory of the gospel to have

Notes: **12:1** Another possible translation for *the sin that so easily entangles* is "the sin which is in good standing" that is, popular or admired by many. Westcott says of this, "The form of the word is favourable to this sense" (1889:393) This meaning would apply equally

on us? A tiny spark of light led them to heaven, but now that the Sun of righteousness shines on us what excuse shall we offer if we still cling to the earth?" Our motivation and inspiration is fuller than theirs, for we have Jesus himself to sustain us. It is to that powerful support that the author now turns his reader's attention.

□ Faith Trained and Tested (12:1-29)

Suddenly the scene shifts to a sports stadium where a distance marathon is being run. The runners are the readers of this epistle (including us), who need to run a grueling race. Encircling the track is a stadium filled with *a great cloud of witnesses,* among them many of the worthies of the past named in chapter 11. They are witnesses in the sense of bearing testimony that the race can be run successfully and that the rewards are great.

The Race of Life (12:1-3) Their encouragement has two purposes: to *throw off everything that hinders* and to put away *the sin that so easily entangles.* As Moses laid aside the prerogatives of royalty for the sake of his God-given mission, so we must throw off whatever may hinder faith even though it may be right for others. Joseph properly ruled in Egypt, but for Moses it was a hindering weight. Other weights might well be ambition, anxieties, hobbies, wealth or fame. Each runner must honestly judge what hinders faith for him or her and resolutely lay it aside, even though others seem to be unhindered by the same thing. One cannot run well in an overcoat!

But the primary block to gaining the prize is *the sin that so easily entangles.* Since the writer does not specify what this is, it may be taken for granted that it is the sin continually warned about in Hebrews—persistent unbelief. Do not take God's Word lightly. Do not excuse any sin as all right for you, but forbidden to others. Do not feel you can evade God's discipline or judgment. Remember: "God cannot be mocked. A man reaps what he sows" (Gal 6:7). Unbelief often looks trivial to us, but Moses was kept out of the Promised Land because he treated God's

---

well to the sin of unbelief, since this is widely approved by a world which easily ignores the word of God, and even by many Christians who take the exhortations of Scripture lightly.

word lightly on one occasion (Deut 32:51-52; Ps 106:33). David apparently felt that his twin sins of adultery and murder could be overlooked because he was king, but God felt otherwise and sent Nathan the prophet to expose his wickedness and to announce his punishment.

The race, of course, is life itself. Since it is God who gives us life, it is also God who starts us in this race. We are all here for a purpose, and that purpose is to live our lives in fulfillment of God's intent for us. This requires not only faith in God's revelation, as we have seen, but also perseverance and endurance. Life is not a 100-yard dash, but a long and sometimes agonizing marathon. No one knows just how long it will be. It can suddenly be cut short, as we have often seen, but its very uncertainty requires that we run it as if it will last a long time, being prepared to keep going no matter what happens. The goal toward which we run is the end of life, whether it be death or the sudden transformation of living saints at the parousia of Jesus (1 Cor 15:51-52). Jesus says to the suffering saints of Smyrna, "Be faithful, even to the point of death, and I will give you the crown of life" (Rev 2:10).

Only one factor can make consistent endurance possible, and this the author states clearly in verse 2: *Let us fix our eyes on Jesus.* This is the central theme of Hebrews. He has stated it before ("But we see Jesus . . ."—2:9; "fix your thoughts on Jesus . . ."—3:1; "since we have a great high priest . . . let us then approach the throne of grace with confidence"—4:14, 16). He is saying, in effect, "Listen to the testimony of those who have gone before for they can help you know what to lay aside; but, above all else, fix your attention on Jesus, for he can do what no one else can—he can impart faith to you, and he can bring it to perfection at the end. He awaits you when you reach the goal, but he is also with you to strengthen your endeavor and guard your steps along the way. Look at other men and women of faith for inspiration and encouragement, but then look higher up to Jesus." This has been well expressed by a Christian poet:

The glory of the light is brightest,
When the glory of self is dim,

12:2 Bruce sees *the joy set before him* as his exaltation at the right hand of the throne of God. However, he adds, "His exaltation there, *with all that it means for His people's well being* and for the triumph of God's purpose, . . . is 'the joy that was set before him' "

And they have most compelled me,
Who most have pointed to Him;
They have held me, stirred me, swayed me—
I have hung on their every word,
'Til I fain would rise and follow,
Not them, not them, but their Lord.

Why look away from human leaders to Jesus? Because he is *the author and perfecter of our faith.* He gives it and completes it. The word translated here "author" is *archēgos,* which we saw in 2:10 has the thought of pioneer or leader. Jesus has gone before us in this race to keep faith. He knows the need for it. He himself ran the race. He laid aside every weight, every tie of family and friends. He set his face against the popular sin of unbelief and daily lived in patient perseverance, trusting his Father to work everything out for him. He set the perfect example. As Bruce says, "It was sheer faith in God, unsupported by any visible evidence, that carried Him through the taunting, the scourging, the crucifying, and the more bitter agony of rejection, desertion and dereliction" (1964:352).

But there is more than example in him—there is also empowerment! Moment by moment, day by day, week by week, year by year, as we look to him, we shall find strength imparted to us. He is not "out there" somewhere. As this epistle has made clear, he is within us, by faith. He has entered into the sanctuary, into the inner person, into the very place where we need strength and grace, and is available every moment to help us in time of need. Having himself lived by faith, he is able to impart that faith to others. He does this by means of the Spirit, as Paul reflects in his prayer of Ephesians 3:16: "I pray that out of his glorious riches he may strengthen you with power through his Spirit in your inner being." This power to awaken faith is what Jesus describes as the enabling of the Father ("no one can come to me unless the Father has enabled him"—Jn 6:65). As the epistle to the Hebrews has repeatedly insisted, faith is essential to spiritual vitality. Jesus is our example of the kind of faith required, but his very life in us imparts the faith we need

(1964:353). Thus he too sees the ministry of Jesus to his people as part of the joy he desired so greatly that he scorned the agony and shame of the Cross.

to run the race of life successfully. So we cry with Paul, "I can do every-thing through him who gives me strength" (Phil 4:13).

This ministry of help for us is undoubtedly *the joy set before him* for which he endured the cross and scorned its shame! It meant more to Jesus than his own well being, even more than the joy of returning to his Father and the glory of heaven. For the consummate joy of "bringing many sons to glory," he gave himself up to agony and death and counted it a small price to pay. It brought him, as verse 2 states, to *sit down at the right hand of the throne of God.* Redemption requires power, and now from the place of ultimate power he can "save completely those who come to God through him."

In Jesus, we have a model to follow which cannot be surpassed, for he, too, patiently endured the opposition of sinful men, even that of his own disciples. But he is also able to impart his own spirit of steadfastness to those who trust him so they *will not grow weary and lose heart!* The author has exhorted us to keep our eyes on Jesus, to *consider him.* He represents faith, which has been tried to the utmost! He could take it because of the strength of his inner life. We, too, can take whatever life throws at us because we have him as our resource to draw upon. No truth in Hebrews is more strongly emphasized than this.

Psychologist Dr. Larry Crabb has described the mentality of many today who look for human help but ignore that offered by our great high priest, Jesus. He says:

> Too often people take a word like *authenticity* and they secularize it to mean, "I'm going to let you know exactly what I feel," thinking that that is going to result in intimacy and a release of guilt.
>
> What may in fact be happening is that you are demanding that the other person now deal with *your* feelings the way *you* want him or her to. If the other person doesn't do that, then you go into hiding convinced that nobody will ever deal with how you really feel; so why bother caring? The point is that you are not facing the real issue. Authenticity demands that you expose yourself not for the purpose of getting a person to respond to you in the way that *you* want, but exposing yourself so *you* can respond to what *God* wants. Only God can truly deal with your sin. Only God can truly forgive you. (Crabb 1989)

How God Trains Us (12:4-13) The passage from verses 4-11 develops the true point of view Christians must have toward hardship and opposition. Verses 4-6 put it succinctly, saying, in effect: Remember, it isn't as bad as it could be! *(You have not yet resisted to the point of shedding your blood.)* Don't forget, behind the difficulties you must go through is a father's loving heart! *(You have forgotten that word of encouragement that addresses you as sons.)* The quotation from Proverbs 3:11-12 is Solomon's words to his own son, helping him to handle the troubles and hardships which will come to him. The Septuagint version quoted here speaks of both rebuke and punishment coming from the Lord. Rebuke is verbal correction; punishment (scourging) is designed to make the rebuke unforgettable. Scourging is severe punishment, symbol ized by the Roman scourge, a leather whip with metal pieces embedded on the end.

An incident from the Old Testament illustrates this. David was rebuked by the Lord for numbering Israel and was given the choice of three punishments. He wisely let the Lord decide, and undoubtedly experienced the least hurtful of the three, but in the plague God sent, 70,000 Israelites died! (2 Sam 24). That was a lesson David never forgot! But it is important to note that our author insists that such discipline comes from God's love for those sons he is bringing to glory. Severe discipline only comes to those who have violated great responsibility or who are being trained for tough assignments. Many Christians today have testified that God got their attention only after some severe trial or circumstance came upon them!

The fact that the severe persecution these Hebrews had already undergone (10:32-33) had not yet involved the shedding of their blood is indication that their location was not Jerusalem or probably even Palestine. Acts records several instances of martyrdom among the early Christians there. But if we are called to follow Christ it may lead to actual bloodshed, as other centuries can bear ample witness, and not least our century! Persecution that stops short of death is something to be thankful for. But discomfort, hardship and deprivations, borne for the sake of Christ, are viewed as privileges and blessings, sent by a loving Father to prepare us to be worthy heirs of the incomparable glories yet to come. They are not a sign of his displeasure, but a sign that he regards us as genuine children.

So, in verses 7-8, the author reminds his readers that they are not illegitimate children for whom no future is being prepared, but legitimate children who require discipline to develop properly. Coach Tom Landry of the Dallas Cowboys is reputed to have said, "The job of a coach is to make men do what they don't want to do, in order to be what they've always wanted to be!" Our author would have welcomed that as an accurate statement of what God does with those he calls to be his children. They should "hang tough" because their trials are proof that they are beloved children and not bastards.

Verses 9-11 adduce a second reason for patient endurance: our earthly fathers disciplined us when we were children, even though they doubtless made mistakes. Yet we respected them for their efforts which we recognized were meant for our good. How much more should we accept the discipline of our God, who makes no mistakes and who aims at enabling us to share his own perfect character! The reference to God as *the Father of our spirits* is meant as a contrast to "human fathers" (Gk "fathers of our flesh") and reminds us that the fruit borne by suffering is spiritual in nature.

The trials, disappointments, hardships and even physical attacks which sometimes constitute God's discipline may be painful to bear. No one *enjoys* such experiences. As C. S. Lewis notes, "God whispers to us in our pleasures, speaks in our conscience, but shouts in our pains: it is His megaphone to arouse a deaf world" (1978:81). But the pain is not the whole story. There is always a *later on* which follows. There is a *harvest of righteousness and peace* which invariably will come *for those who have been trained by it* (the discipline).

Christian suffering is not simply sheer circumstantial misery or the result of blind chance. Paul declares, "We know that suffering produces perseverance; perseverance, character; and character, hope" (Rom 5:3-4). James adds, "You know that the testing of your faith develops perseverance. Perseverance must finish its work so that you may be mature and complete, not lacking anything" (Jas 1:3-4). Peter concurs, "These [trials] have come so that your faith—of greater worth than gold, which perishes even though refined by fire—may be proved genuine and may result in praise, glory and honor when Jesus Christ is revealed" (1 Pet

1:7). How foolish then it is to complain and grouse about the difficulties we face. "If we are always rebelling against it and refusing to learn the lessons the Father is teaching us, we are shutting ourselves up to discontent and misunderstanding" (Morris 1983:123).

Our author well understands the tendency we all have to reject well-intentioned advice and concentrate on our misery. We derive a kind of perverse pleasure from so doing. So he urges, in verses 12-13, two specific actions:

1. *Strengthen your feeble arms and weak knees.* That is, deal first with yourselves. Get your own hearts right toward your troubles. He has already pointed out the way to do so: by each coming boldly to the throne of grace "so that we may receive mercy and find grace to help us in our time of need" (4:16). He has said the same in 12:2: "Let us fix our eyes on Jesus, the author and perfecter of our faith." It is only as we know his help ourselves that we are able to aid anyone else in finding it. The plural imperative *(strengthen,* Gk "lift up") implies a joint effort by many. We can help each other draw upon the resources of Christ by offering encouraging words and mutual prayers, sharing our experiences and sometimes simply being with someone who is undergoing trial.

2. *Make level paths for your feet, so that the lame may not be disabled, but rather healed.* That is, watch your influence on others! Take care that you are not a stumbling block to those who travel with you, whose faith may be much weaker than yours. *Disabled* carries the thought of having something thrown out of joint, as in a sprain or twist.

The two exhortations look back to Isaiah 35:4 where the prophet exhorts: "Say to those with fearful hearts, 'Be strong, do not fear; your God will come, he will come with vengeance; with divine retribution he will come to save you.' " This is not only an exhortation to wait patiently for the coming of Christ (10:37) but also to expect God to "come" in some sovereign action of deliverance in response to his people's prayers. Acts 12 records such a deliverance in the case of Peter whom Herod had put in prison. Any degree of persecution should be met by the Christian body gathering in mutual support so that no one is spiritually disabled. It is necessary to be strong for the sake of others as well as ourselves. The way we bear suffering has enormous impact on the whole Christian community, and the author stresses this point with this in view.

The Dangers to Watch For (12:14-17) This concern for others leads to a more general exhortation to the whole community of faith in verses 14-24. Each member pursues two objectives: peace with all men and holiness before God. As Paul suggests in Romans 12:18, to live at peace with all is not always possible, but it must be pursued "as far as it depends on you!" The causing of strife should never begin with a believer! Here Paul's practical suggestions found in 1 Corinthian 6:1-8 are apropos. Disputes ought to be settled by arbitration rather than lawsuits. Seeking counsel is preferable to hurling charges, and forbearance is most fitting for those whom God has forgiven. How many disgraceful public displays of church disagreements could be prevented if this admonition of 12:14 were heeded.

But of even more importance is the pursuit of holiness, for without it *no one will see the Lord.* Whether this seeing of the Lord refers to the beatific vision of God (Bruce 1964:364), or to seeing Jesus at his Second Coming (Westcott 1889:406), it clearly precludes any who are not pursuing holiness from having a close and vital relationship with God. The need to *make every effort* suggests continuance and is perhaps better translated "pursue." As we have noted before, it is a mistake to take holiness as referring only to righteous behavior apart from seeing it also as a gift of God who imparts righteousness to the one who believes in Jesus.

If we pursue righteous behavior only as a means to "seeing" the Lord, we will eventually find ourselves with the Pharisees. They were blindly ignorant of terrible failure but claimed a relationship that did not really exist. But if we truly practice a continual reckoning of ourselves as already righteous within by a gracious act of God on the basis of the death and resurrection of Jesus, we will find ourselves strongly motivated to live righteously and inwardly distressed at any failure to do so. This inward distress will bring us again and again to the throne of grace for forgiveness and recovery. We will progressively be "transformed into his (Christ's) likeness with ever-increasing glory, which comes from the Lord, who is the Spirit" (2 Cor 3:18). That is what is meant by the exhortation to "pursue holiness, without which no man shall see the Lord" (KJV).

A failure to do this is called, in verse 15, missing the grace of God. The writer has already warned of this in 3:12: "See to it, brothers, that none of you has a sinful, unbelieving heart that turns away from the living God." Such unbelief is a bitter root which will create strife and defile many. The root is unbelief which refuses to reckon on God's provision of righteousness because it feels confident it can produce an acceptable righteousness on its own. Strife and defilement are the bitter fruit which this root inevitably produces. It will reveal itself in two forms: sexual immorality or godlessness, like that of Esau. The first is defilement of the body; the second is defilement of the soul. Our author only touches on the first at this point but will bring it up again at 13:4. Yet this brief reference must not be missed for it equates sexual immorality in its effects with a godless spirit.

The author uses Esau to illustrate the second form. The word for godlessness is *bebēlos,* which is best translated "profane" or, as we would say, "secular." It is a mindset which takes little notice of anything beyond the material. This was Esau's outlook (Gen 27:30-40). He thought so little of the promises of God to Abraham and Isaac, to which he was the primary heir as the firstborn, that he sold those rights to his brother Jacob for a bowl of stew! So unimportant was this transaction in his eyes that later he assumed he could still receive the blessing which accompanied the right of firstborn. Though his brother Jacob had tricked their blind father into conferring the blessing upon himself, Esau still tried to change his father's words and gain the blessing he had sold. His father could not and would not change his mind, so Esau lost both the birthright and the blessing.

That is the secular mentality. It has little time for worship or service, but it is intent upon material gain and earthly advantage. Professing Christians who claim to be born again but who live no differently than non-Christians are repeating the godlessness of Esau. Like him they too will find a surprising rejection in the last day. Jesus has them in mind when he says, "Then I will tell them plainly, 'I never knew you. Away from me, you evildoers!' " (Mt 7:23).

The Blessings Now Possible (12:18-24) The author has, throughout the letter, been drawing a contrast between the old covenant of the law, which was given at Mount Sinai, and the new covenant of grace, which actually preceded the law. It was made fully manifest in the ministry and sacrifice of Jesus. Now, in verses 18-24, he repeats the contrast using striking symbols, drawing from Exodus and Deuteronomy the fearful scene at Mount Sinai when the Ten Commandments were given, and from the prophets various elements of the heavenly Jerusalem which are associated with the new covenant.

The point of his description of Mount Sinai and the giving of the law is that the old covenant aroused unbearable fear. The sight of the burning mountain and the ever-increasing blare of a trumpet, the darkness, storm and fearful threats directed even toward dumb beasts, created such fear in the people that they begged Moses to plead with God for relief. Even Moses said, "I am trembling with fear." That is the invariable end of efforts made to obey a law which requires perfection. Fear of God's just condemnation is overwhelming. Most people do not feel this fear because they do not take the law seriously, at least not until they reach the end of their lives and its fearful judgments lie immediately before them. All who seek earnestly to obey the law find themselves confronted with such personal failure that they soon despair of escaping God's fearful condemnation. Mount Sinai stands as the symbol of this despair and fear.

"For what the law was powerless to do . . . God did by sending his own Son in the likeness of sinful man to be a sin offering" (Rom 8:3). That is the triumphant cry of the new covenant! Our author's description of it (vv. 22-24) is one of joyful celebration. It consists of six elements.

1. *You have come to Mount Zion, to the heavenly Jerusalem, the city of the living God.* That is the same city which Abraham and the patriarchs sought (11:10, 16). It is what Paul called "Jerusalem that is above" (Gal 4:26), mother to all believers. Our author views it as already attained by those who have believed the new covenant and come to Jesus. In spirit they were residents of the city already, though in body they were yet pilgrims and strangers on earth. That there is yet to be an earthly manifestation of the city is clear from the later reference in 13:13 to "the city which is yet to come."

2. *You have come to thousands upon thousands of angels in joyful assembly.* The myriads of angels are referred to several times in Scripture

(Deut 33:2; Dan 7:10; Lk 2:13; Rev 5:11). All of these six elements here
are governed by the verb translated, "you have come" (*proselēlythate*).
The perfect tense indicates a condition already existent with continuing
effect. The thought of the author here is probably that of 1:14: "Are not
all angels ministering spirits sent to serve those who will inherit salvation?" Angels minister, with joy, to believers in many hidden ways, helping them run the race of life with patient endurance. An example of this
is found in Acts 27:23-24.

3. You have come *to the church of the firstborn, whose names are
written in heaven.* Bruce properly sees this as a reference to the whole
communion of saints who have come, not merely into the presence of
the church, but into its membership by faith in Christ (1964:376-377).
The writing of their names in heaven recalls Jesus' words to his disciples,
"Rejoice that your names are written in heaven" (Lk 10:20). They share
with Jesus the title of firstborn (Col 1:18) because they are "heirs of God
and coheirs with Christ" (Rom 8:17).

4. *You have come to God, the judge of all men.* The Greek text properly
reads, "to a judge, who is God of all men." Without exception, all humans must stand before God to be judged. But the glory of the gospel
is that believers may stand before him without fear, since Jesus himself
assures each one that he "has eternal life and will not be condemned;
he has crossed over from death to life" (Jn 5:24). This relief from the
fear of judgment is an enormous blessing to those who know themselves
to be sinners in word, thought and deed.

5. You have come *to the spirits of righteous men made perfect.* Commentators have differed over whether this describes "believers of pre-
Christian days" (Bruce) or "New Testament believers" (Bengel). It likely
looks back to 11:40 and the Old Testament saints who would be made
perfect "together with us." Since it is their spirits which have been made
perfect and not their bodies, it suggests that these saints, who lived
before the Cross, are waiting with us for the resurrection to come. Jesus
spoke to the Jews of "other sheep [Gentiles] that are not of this sheep
pen." "They too," he added, "will listen to my voice, and there shall be
one flock and one shepherd" (Jn 10:16). As we have already noted, when
the heavenly Jerusalem comes to earth, as John sees it in Revelation 21:2,
these words will be fulfilled. Its gates are named for the twelve tribes

of Israel, and its foundation stones bear the names of the twelve apostles of the Lamb.

6. You have come *to Jesus the mediator of a new covenant, and to the sprinkled blood that speaks a better word than the blood of Abel.* Moses was the mediator of the old covenant and under it, the Aaronic priests sprinkled blood upon the mercy seat to cover over the sins of Israel. This made the continued presence of God among them possible. As our author has ably shown, all this was but a shadow of the new covenant where Jesus would be an eternal mediator, sprinkling his own blood which does not merely cover over sins but take them entirely away. The *better word* of which his blood speaks is forgiveness, whole and complete. This is in contrast to the blood of Abel, which, as we saw earlier, could only call for vindication but could not offer forgiveness. Let us never forget that we are redeemed, not with perishable things such as silver or gold "but with the precious blood of Christ, a lamb without blemish or defect" (1 Pet 1:19).

To summarize, the advantages of being in Christ consist of (1) living already, in spirit, in the new Jerusalem which Abraham and Old Testament believers longed to see; (2) joining already in praise around the throne of God with myriads of the heavenly host; (3) belonging to a body of believers who are members with each other and who share a heavenly citizenship; (4) having no fear of God's judgment even though standing spiritually before his august throne; (5) sharing with Old Testament believers the certain hope of the resurrection of the body; and (6) possessing Jesus in a new and intimate relationship ("you in me and I in you"), which involves a complete and final solution of the problem of human sin.

The Fifth and Final Warning (12:25-29) Since believers in Christ now possess such enormous resources for living as those just described, it is of the utmost importance to act in accordance with them. Truth simply understood is never acceptable in and of itself; it is truth done that counts! So, for the fifth time in this epistle, the author warns against turning back from the truth they have learned as professing Christians to a more comfortable and less demanding life in Judaism or to an accommodation to the unbelieving lifestyles around them.

Verses 25-27 take us back to the first warning of 2:1-3. There the Hebrews were in danger of drifting away from that which they had heard; here they also stand in peril of refusing *him who speaks.* There they were reminded that violations of the law received immediate punishment; here they are also told that those who refused the One who gave commandments from the mountain *did not escape.* There the question confronted them: "How shall we escape if we ignore such a great salvation?" Here the question is *How much less will we [escape], if we turn away from him who warns us from heaven?* There the message was one "spoken by angels," in contrast to the salvation "first announced by the Lord." Here the contrast is also between the message spoken *on earth* from the mountain, and the word which has come to them from him who speaks *from heaven* (which almost certainly refers to 1:1-2: "God . . . has spoken to us by his Son").

It is clear that the warning passages envision the same peril—that apathy toward spiritual matters and complacency with a religious lifestyle falls far short of what God requires and has made full provision for. But such complacency cannot go unjudged forever. It actually constitutes a refusal of God's grace, a turning of one's back on truth and deliverance. This is where some, if not many, of the recipients of this letter now stand. The last three warnings particularly (6:4-6; 10:26-31 and here) envision a deliberate and final rejection of the new covenant as the greatest danger. The shaking of Mount Sinai was designed to arouse serious consideration of the demands of the law on the Israelites. Since such "earthly" shaking was not sufficient to gain their full attention a greater shaking is yet to come; a shaking not merely of earth but of earth and heaven together.

We have already noted that heaven is the realm of invisible realities, of forces and principles which actually govern human life. The word translated "created things" *(pepoiēmenōn)* means "things made," but 11:2 reminds us that behind the visible things are invisible forces. This shaking of heaven and earth is both of the visible and of the invisible. Isaiah also declares: "Therefore I will make the heavens tremble; and the earth will shake from its place at the wrath of the LORD Almighty, in the day of his burning anger" (Is 13:13). It is this greater shaking from which there is no escape. That shaking began with the preaching of Jesus (Hag

2:6) has been continuing through the Christian centuries, and will culminate in the great judgments described in Daniel and Revelation. The earth and heaven will flee away and be replaced by the new heavens and the new earth.

There is something chilling about the thought of a shaking of heaven and earth. The twentieth century has watched the crumbling of much which we once thought to be stable. Faith in human government has been widely shaken; confidence in science as the savior of the race has waned as the problems of pollution, urban decay, biological warfare and existential despair increase. Long-accepted moral standards have disappeared under the onslaught of divorce, unmarriages, sexual explicitness, homosexuality and abortion.

But there are some things which cannot be shaken and which will remain forever. That which is shaken and removed is so done in order that what cannot be shaken may stand revealed. Such an unshakable thing is the kingdom of God into which those who trust in Jesus have entered. It is present wherever the King is honored, loved and obeyed. The present active participle ("are receiving") indicates a continuing process. We enter the kingdom at conversion, but we abide in it daily as we reckon upon the resources which come to us from our invisible but present King. Such unbroken supply should arouse a continuing sense of gratitude within us and lead to acceptable worship of God. What renders such worship acceptable is the sense of God as incredibly powerful and majestic in person, and yet loving and compassionate of heart. An old hymn puts it well:

Immortal, invisible, God only wise,

In light inaccessible, hid from our eyes.

How blessed, how glorious, the Ancient of Days

Almighty, Victorious, thy great name we praise!

The proper attitude of Christians must be one of awe that a Being of such majesty and glory could find a way to dwell eternally with such sin-controlled and sin-injured creatures as us. Since our *"God is a consuming fire,"* we must cry with Isaiah, "Who of us can dwell with the consuming fire? Who of us can dwell with everlasting burning?" (Is 33:14). God's love is just such a fire, it destroys what it cannot purify, but purifies what it cannot destroy. In Jesus we have a relationship that cannot be destroyed (Rom 8:38-39). Our great king is leading us through trials and difficulties in order that we may at last cry with Job, "He knows the way that I take; when he has tried me, I shall come forth as gold" (Job 23:10 KJV).

☐ Faith at Work (13:1-25)

If you like to get letters from close, loving friends you will enjoy this last chapter of Hebrews for it affects us as much as it did its original readers. The great pastoral heart of the writer comes to the fore in his closing words. Far from being an unrelated addendum, written perhaps by another hand or at another time as some commentators have claimed, the chapter is a natural close for one who has finished his teaching and warnings and now gives some final words of loving application. One by one, he touches on the kinds of behavior by Christians which will impress a secularized society with the value and power of Christian truth. The general acceptance of religious pluralism in America has made standard methods of Christian witness less and less effective. Christians are now being judged, not on their teachings, but on their lives. What qualities of life will favorably influence the Buddhist family down the street, or the Vietnamese who moved into the neighborhood, or the young unmarried couple who live together in the apartment downstairs, who are turned off by church and know next to nothing about the Bible? This first-century author confronts the same kind of pluralistic world with urgings that work in any age.

Keep Love and Purity Central (13:1-6) First, and above all else, is brotherly love (v. 1). Jesus himself said this would be the mark by which his true disciples would be known (Jn 13:35). It is not a love based on personal liking, but one based on a shared relationship. All Christians are "members one of another" because they share the life of Christ. They value and care for each other because they are brothers and sisters, whether they naturally like each other or not. In 12:12-17, the author has already shown his concern that his readers guard their influence on other believers and strive to live at peace, avoiding immorality and a materialistic spirit. Here he indicates the more positive side of actively showing love. There is a practical quality to this love, as 1 John 3:17 indicates:

"If anyone has material possessions and sees his brother in need but has no pity on him, how can the love of God be in him?" Church members then checked up on those in need and saw to it that their basic needs for food, shelter and clothing were met.

Second, they were to be hospitable and generous, even with total strangers or any who showed need of their ministrations. Job could say, "No stranger had to spend the night in the street, for my door was always open to the traveler" (Job 31:32). Certain Old Testament saints, because of their hospitable ways, had enjoyed extraordinary experiences with angelic visitors. Noteworthy among them would be Abraham (Gen 18), Gideon (Judg 6) and Manoah (Judg 13). Hospitality to strangers is a peculiarly significant mark of Christian ministry since it reflects the undeserving mercy which the Christian has received from God already. Jesus said, "Freely you have received, freely give" (Mt 10:8), and warm hospitality reflects such an attitude. Such hospitality is not manifest in the modern practice of repaying entertainment by one's friends, though that is not wrong in itself. It is simply not reaching out to strangers as Jesus commanded (Lk 14:13-14). Fear, lest one be taken advantage of, keeps many from this practice, but first-century believers found a way to minimize that. An early Christian commentary, the *Didache,* limited visits to only one day, or two if necessary. If a Christian stayed three days, he was regarded as a false prophet (Bruce 1964:390).

A third display of true Christian concern is to become aware of the needs of prisoners and others suffering difficult circumstances. Empathy is called for, not merely help. We must feel with the prisoner or the mistreated, the shame, hurt and hopelessness they often experience, and minister to them out of an awareness that we too could have been where they are, had our circumstances been the same as theirs. Even those imprisoned justly merit Christian help, since Jesus ministered to the guilty and the condemned simply because they were human beings, who were victims of self-deceit or ignorance. Churches in the twentieth cen-

Notes: 13:2 Perhaps a caution should be added in this violent age against a mechanical or legalistic practice of this exhortation. Due care should be exercised with strangers to guard against admitting those with criminal intent to a home or those who habitually prey upon ingenuous people. There should be clear evidence of the need of hospitality, and wisdom exercised in perhaps including other trusted persons.

tury have too easily shifted concern for the poor and homeless to the shoulders of government. That help should be welcomed, but it must be remembered that it will often be rather impersonal and short-lived. Christians can add dimensions of love and continuance that non-Christians are not capable of showing. Each Christian should frequently review his or her efforts in this direction, for these exhortations are still valid today.

As a fourth indication of Christian reality, marriage must be preserved as God-given and honorable, with no sexual infidelity tolerated. This second reference to the danger of sexual immorality indicates the concern on this point in early Christian teaching. They saw clearly that marriage cannot exist where sexual infidelity is tolerated. But even failure in this area would not call for cold condemnation. Counsel, understanding, and a willingness to forgive and restore upon repentance are needed.

The family is the basic unit of society, and any breakdown soon begins to affect all. We are witnessing the truth of this widely today. Laxity among Christians is probably responsible for the attitude of many young people who regard marriage as "just a scrap of paper" and feel free to live together without benefit of marriage vows. The point to remember is that God views infidelity as serious and will allow the natural consequences of pain, hurt and guilt to take their terrible toll, and no way can be found to escape it. It is in this way that he judges *the adulterer and all the sexually immoral.* The knowledge of such inevitable consequences should induce couples to work hard at solving marriage rifts and to seek spiritual help in fleeing from temptations to sexual sin. Christian leaders must see that such help is available and that it is not superficial or inaccurate. The moral climate of society may regard biblical sexual standards as quaint and old-fashioned, but the church especially ought to hold to such standards in a time of declension.

The fifth sign of genuine Christian life is a contented, greed-free at-

13:5-6 The Greek phrases for "Never will I leave you; never will I forsake you" constitute the strongest expression of assurance possible. They may be interpreted: "Never, under any circumstances ever, will I leave you!" God promises to supply, as Paul stoutly avers (Phil 4:19), but believers must allow him to do so in his own way and time, without specifying either.

titude (vv. 5-6). The basis for such contentment is God's promise and ability to supply the necessities of life (Mt 6:25-34). Loving money must particularly be avoided as it becomes a substitute for faith in God's loving care and induces a false trust in an unreliable supply. God has said he will never leave us nor forsake us. This should evoke, "The Lord is my helper; I will not be afraid. What can man do to me?" The two quotations, one from Deuteronomy 31:6 and the other from Psalm 118:6-7, reveal that the answer to any kind of fear, including the fear of poverty, is found in the commitment of God to ever be with us. There are many warnings in Scripture against loving money. Jesus said it was impossible to serve both God and money, and Paul had written young Timothy: "People who want to get rich fall into temptation and a trap and into many foolish and harmful desires that plunge men into ruin and destruction" (1 Tim 6:9).

Though credit cards were unknown in the first century, they often constitute a trap today that results in financial ruin and destruction. The point of danger is the love of money which cancels out the sense of God's love and promised supply, and launches the believer into worldly schemes for financial security that belie all trust in God. This is not to set aside the recognition that God can and often does supply methods of financial support using banks, insurance, securities and other means. But all these must be seen as coming from his hand. It is always spiritually dangerous to grow financially discontent. Remember Paul's words: "Some people, eager for money, have wandered from the faith and pierced themselves with many griefs" (1 Tim 6:10).

Life in the Church (13:7-19) The five manifestations listed above are normal expressions of the new life in Christ. They are open to all true believers and, when consistently exhibited, are designed to impress non-Christians with the advantages of faith. In the next section, from verses 7-19, the author focuses more on the marks of faith at work within the

---

13:10 Is the *altar* mentioned here a reference to the Lord's Supper, commonly called the Eucharist? Many have thought so through the centuries. Though it is natural to tie this to the Lord's words in John 6:53-54 ("Unless you eat the flesh of the Son of Man and drink his blood, you have no life in you. Whoever eats my flesh and drinks my blood has eternal life"), it cannot be demonstrated that the writer of Hebrews has this in mind. To take it as a direct reference to the Eucharist has given strength to the concept of the Mass, which views the bread and wine as transformed into the body and blood of Christ. But the early church

life of the church. Prominent among these is respect for and compliance with godly leaders (mentioned three times in this chapter—vv 7, 17, 24). Here, the aorist *elalēsan* ("spoke") indicates leaders who were no longer with them, who probably had died, and yet the impress of their lives is still on those who remain.

It is particularly their faith that must be emulated, since it was fixed on Jesus who is unchangeable and always available. Almost every Christian has some mentor who has shaped his or her faith by godly example, and their memory is a continual encouragement to draw strength from the unchanging Lord. The memorial marker to John Wesley in Westminster Abbey bears the inscription: "God buries his workmen, but he carries on his work." Memories of godly lives help best when they turn us to the One who never needs to be replaced and who is permanently available to his people. This great statement that Jesus is unchanged and unchangeable builds upon 1:10-12 where all creation may pass away but Jesus the Creator remains forever the same. Here, at the end of Hebrews, Jesus' role as mediator of the new covenant and pioneer of faith who is always available to his people is even more the focal point of the author's declaration.

The section of verses 9-12 is directed against the tendency of many Christians then and now to seek approval or status from God by eating, or refraining from eating, certain special foods. The once-held Catholic practice of eating fish on Friday would be a case in point. Many appeals are made today for vegetarianism, special diets, and even the use of marijuana, peyote or other hallucinogenic drugs, which are designed to enhance spiritual vitality. The author calls such practices *all kinds of strange teachings* and warns against becoming involved with such beliefs. They turn attention from the strengthening by grace which trust in the living Christ can bring to the troubled heart. For, in any case, the ascetic practices of some have done them no good, for the author asserts

Fathers did not view this as the Eucharist, for it is not till Cyprian, in the third century, "that it [the altar] begins to be used as a synonym for the Lord's table" (Hughes 1977:578). Even Thomas Aquinas states: "This altar is either the cross of Christ, on which Christ was sacrificed for us, or Christ himself, in whom and through whom we offer our prayers" (Hughes 1977:578). Though the Lord's Supper presents a magnificent occasion to inwardly feed upon the value of Christ's sacrifice for us, it is probably not what was in the mind of the author of Hebrews.

they are *of no value to those who eat them.* It brings to mind Paul's word to the Colossians: "Such regulations indeed have an appearance of wisdom, with their self-imposed worship, their false humility and their harsh treatment of the body, but they lack any value in restraining sensual indulgence" (Col 2:23). Churches should frequently alert their people against involvement in such useless practices.

In the words *we have an altar from which those who minister at the tabernacle have no right to eat* the author is still seeking to direct faith to the person of Jesus, instead of some empty ritual. This is made clear in verse 11, where he refers to the sin offering of the Day of Atonement. He thinks of Christ's sacrifice as the antitype of that sin offering, and it is that antitype which constitutes the altar we Christians have. It is, of course, the Cross. The priests of Israel could not eat the flesh of any animal whose blood was sprinkled on the mercy seat, though they partook freely of the flesh of other sacrificed animals. The bodies of the sin offerings were burnt *outside the camp* where Jesus was also taken when he was crucified (Jn 19:20 "near the city"). Though the priests had no right to eat of the bodies of the sin offerings, we do have the right to nourish ourselves on the life of our great Sin Offering, Jesus. We are "eating Christ" when we trust him and obey him. This may be an oblique reference to the words of Jesus in John 6:53-54 ("Unless you eat the flesh of the Son of Man and drink his blood, you have no life in you. Whoever eats my flesh and drinks my blood has eternal life, and I will raise him up at the last day"), though this cannot be certain. But to draw grace and strength from Jesus is to be made holy daily. This is on the basis of the once-for-all shedding of Jesus' blood. It was for this very purpose that Jesus suffered outside the city gate.

So the appeal comes again: *Let us, then, go to him outside the camp, bearing the disgrace he bore* (v. 13). The word for *disgrace* is the same word used of Moses in 11:26, who chose to bear reproach for the sake of Christ. The camp is the religious establishment, whether of Judaism or of a distorted Christianity. Going outside that camp does not necessarily mean a physical withdrawal. It refers more to the inner attitude which sees no value in religious ritual and dietary restrictions. It looks directly to the promises of the new covenant for personal strength to live by. There is a recognition here that visible religious practices are often highly regarded by society at large, and those who live by faith, without the need for impressive buildings, rituals, altars, vestments and the like, are often scorned as having nothing beautiful about their faith to commend it. The scorners have forgotten, of course, the admonition of Scripture: "Worship the LORD in the splendor of holiness" (Ps 29:2). God has never made anything more beautiful than a genuinely holy person whose inner commitment and fellowship with Christ is visibly evidenced by a loving spirit, a humble attitude, a forgiving heart and a moral walk.

This lack of need for materially expressed religion is underscored by the author in verse 14: *For here we do not have an enduring city, but we are looking for the city that is to come.* Like Abraham of old, believers are pilgrims and strangers in the world, looking forward, as he did, to "the city with foundations, whose architect and builder is God" (11:10). This is not intended to sentence believers of every age to penury— for Abraham was rich—or to prohibit involvement with politics or business—for Abraham was involved in both. But it frees us from lusting after material benefits, and especially from seeking to gain influence by religious display. We have already attained to that "city that is to come" in our spirits (12:22); we shall enter it in body at the resurrection when Jesus returns (Rev 21:2-4). We are in no need now of ornate buildings, special ceremonies and elaborate ritual.

How is true faith then to be manifested? Verses 15-16 answer with the sacrifices of genuine praise, and compassionate sharing and help. Worship and service: these are the fruits produced by genuine life from God. They are to be done *through Jesus,* and *continually* (Gk *dia pantos,* through everything), because it is with such sacrifices (not by empty rituals) that God is pleased (Is 58:6-9 and Hos 6:6). James agrees with this, "Religion that God our Father accepts as pure and faultless is this: to look after orphans and widows in their distress and to keep oneself from being polluted by the world" (Jas 1:27). The worship of Christians together and their practical deeds of compassion and help are the "sacrifices" with which God is pleased. A Christian poet expresses this perfectly:

'Tis in the daily toil and stress
  we best can preach his loveliness,
It's Mrs. Johnston's shining face proclaims

that she is saved by grace,
While Mrs. Smith by kindly deeds
   shows how from sin her soul is freed
And in the busy common round
   reveals the Saviour she has found.
And Ann by polishing the floors
   tells forth the Master she adores.
"Oh, Lord," I pray on bended knee,
   "make me like these, thy children, please."

In 13:7, the author recalled to his reader's minds the influence for good left by mentors who were now gone. In verse 17, he urges respect for and compliance with the godly leaders they now have. This verse, along with 1 Thessalonians 5:12, has been widely misunderstood because of the faulty translation of the KJV, NIV and other versions. The words *obey* (twice here) and *submit* and the phrase from 1 Thessalonians 5:12 "are over you in the Lord" have often fueled a harmful authoritarianism that has turned pastors into autocrats and congregations into personal domains. Such a twisted view of authority ignores entirely Jesus' words to the disciples: "You know that those who are supposed to rule over the Gentiles lord it over them, and their great men exercise authority over them. *But it shall not be so among you:* but whoever would be great among you must be your servant" (Mk 10:42-43 RSV).

Perhaps those words, "it shall not be so among you," have been among the most ignored sayings of Jesus within the churches. Wherever leadership views itself as having God-given authority to impose rules or limitations on individual Christians or a congregation without their willing consent, these words of Jesus are being violated. Warnings against "lording it over the brethren" are given in 2 Corinthians 1:24 by Paul, in 1 Peter 5:3 by Peter, and in 3 John 9-10 by John.

The author's basis for urging his readers to give willing response to their leaders is that the leaders are godly men who feel deeply their

13:17 Several things should be noted about Hebrews 13:17 and 1 Thessalonians 5:12. The word "obey" comes from the Greek *peithō*, "to persuade." The present imperative middle form, used here, means "permit oneself to be persuaded," "yield to persuasion." It definitely does not mean to blindly follow orders. The phrase *those who are over you in the Lord* should simply be "your leaders in the Lord." There is no thought of being "over"

responsibility to lead wisely and lovingly *as men who must give an account.* This account must be given, not to the congregation, but to the Lord (1 Pet 5:2-4). Henri J. M. Nouwen has said, "The task of future Christian leaders is not to make a little contribution to the solution of the pains and tribulations of their time, but to identify and announce the ways in which Jesus is leading God's people out of slavery, through the desert to a new land of freedom. Christian leaders have the arduous task of responding to personal struggles, family conflicts, national calamities, and international tensions with an articulate faith in God's real presence." If individuals yield voluntary submission to such responsible leadership, it will make the leader's work a joy and of great advantage to all. Note that the responsibility for making the operations of a church a joy, and not a burden, is placed on the congregation, not on their leaders. Even the Declaration of Independence recognizes that legitimate government derives its just powers from the consent of the governed!

The closing section of the epistle takes a more personal turn. Still thinking of leaders and their need of support from those they lead, the writer asks his readers to pray for him (vv. 18-19) and bestows on them a benediction of unusual power and beauty (vv. 20-21). His prayer request concerns his own desire to live in good conscience and to be able soon to come for a personal visit. There may be a veiled awareness here of some possible resentment in his readers for the blunt things he had to say to them or for his long absence from them. But he does not feel that he did anything wrong in speaking bluntly *(we are sure that we have a clear conscience),* and he enlists their prayerful concern that he may visit them again soon. Any resentment on their part would surely be dispelled by the warmth of his closing benediction.

A Gathered-Together Prayer (13:20-21) Verses 20-21 must rank among the most powerfully worded blessings found in the Scripture.

anyone, or others being "under" a leader. The authority of a Christian leader is not command authority, but servant leadership. A servant has authority, as Jesus said he had, because he awakens by his loving service a desire to comply. Or he is persuasive because of his logic or knowledge.

They gather up the passionate concern of the writer for his readers' spiritual growth and stress the major factors that make such growth possible: the God of peace, the blood of the eternal covenant, the resurrection of Jesus, his Shepherd care for his sheep, the indwelling life of God himself, the equipping of the Spirit, the aim to please God, and the eternal glory and lordship of Jesus. It is all there in one glorious outpouring of good wishes and confident certainty.

Bruce sees it as a kind of collect (a gathered-together prayer) which later became popular in the Latin churches. These are the themes of Hebrews, brilliantly restated and forming an appropriate conclusion to the letter. The *God of peace* is surely a reference to the peace given to all who are justified by faith (Rom 5:1); the *blood of the eternal covenant* recalls all the writer has said in chapters 8—10 about the opening of a new and living way to God; *brought back from the dead our Lord Jesus,* though the only direct reference to the resurrection in the epistle, implies the new beginning and the new power which is now shared with all who believe; *that great Shepherd of the sheep* pictures the high-priestly ministry of Jesus under a different figure; *equip you with everything good* speaks of the spiritual gifts imparted by the Spirit, mentioned in 2:4; *work[ing] in us what is pleasing to him* looks back to 13:15-16, the worship and service of God's people; and *through Jesus Christ, to whom be glory for ever and ever* concludes with the pre-eminent theme of the entire letter: the superiority of Jesus to anything and everything else that men worship or honor.

With such marvelous resources as these, who can excuse any failure to become the man or woman God intends you to be? We may well adopt for our own the words of J. I. Packer: "My task is not to dizzy myself by introspecting or speculating to find (if I can) what lies at the outer reaches of consciousness, nor to pursue endless, exquisite stimulation in the hope of new exotic ecstasies. It is, rather, to know and keep my place in God's cosmic hierarchy, and in that place to spend my strength in serving God and men" (1986:67-68).

Closing Words (13:22-25) The final verses (vv. 22-25) continue the note of affection in the address *brothers* and in the plea to take his *word of exhortation* in a well-meant sense. It is relatively short compared with what he could have said had he fully developed his themes (compare 5:11 and 9:5). Certainly *all* commentaries on Hebrews are much longer than the letter itself! The writer's own view of his message is that he is simply fulfilling the same ministry he urges upon his readers in 3:13, "But encourage [same Gk word as *exhort*] one another daily, as long as it is called Today, so that none of you may be hardened by sin's deceitfulness." This passionate concern for their spiritual welfare has been expressed throughout the letter.

He announces to his friends that Timothy has now been released, presumably from prison, and may be able to join him on his proposed visit to their locality. Nothing further is known of Timothy's imprisonment, though it suggests that Paul's warning to him in 2 Timothy 4:15 to be on his guard against Alexander the metalworker was not without substance. It may well be that Alexander obtained Timothy's incarceration, and if so, it would probably have been at Ephesus. Timothy would have had many friends throughout the province of Asia, and it is likely that the recipients of this letter live somewhere in that area, or in a neighboring province such as Phrygia or Galatia. The greetings extended from *those from Italy* do not mean that Hebrews was written from Italy, for then the writer would have said "those in (or of) Italy." The phrase designates a group of Italians now living wherever the writer is when he writes.

He asks his readers to greet their leaders for him, indicating that the letter was not addressed to the leaders themselves but to the church at large, including possibly some home churches *(all God's people)*. This is the third mention of leaders within this chapter, showing the author's respect for their position and value. The closing *Grace be with you all* is another indication of his close association with Paul, for this is identical with the ending of the letter to Titus (3:15), and the conferring of grace is Paul's habitual way of closing his letters (2 Thess 3:17).

This letter was written at a time when the winds of change were blowing strongly throughout the Roman Empire, and most strongly within Judaism. At such times humans tend to cling to familiar patterns and resist change simply because it is unfamiliar and therefore threatening. But their real need is for recognition of the things which cannot change and receptivity toward the things which must be changed. Bruce well states the case: "Every fresh movement of the Spirit of God tends to become stereotyped in the next generation, and what we have heard with our ears, what our fathers have told us, becomes a tenacious tradition encroaching on the allegiance which ought to be accorded only to the living and active word of God" (1964:416).

The epistle to the Hebrews magnificently links the things which cannot be shaken with the fresh sweep of the Spirit in carrying forward the purposes of God as history moves toward its predicted consummation. It is a document greatly needed as the world lurches toward judgment and a new creation, based on the new covenant, gradually emerges from the crashing chaos of human events. Let us be grateful for its wise and careful teaching and obedient to its passionate concern for a constantly maturing faith.

APPENDIX: Some Further Reflections on Hebrews 6

Can spiritual life be lost once it has been received? That is a question which has divided Christians for centuries. An imposing list of scriptural references can be made to support either a yes or a no. But both cannot be right—unless the problem is our limited understanding of God's process of salvation! Perhaps our situation is not unlike that of the five blind men in Aesop's fable who each took hold of a different part of an elephant and insisted the whole must be similar to only the part they could feel. Let us take another tack and see if it helps to understand the issue.

Scripture frequently uses the analogy of physical birth and growth to picture spiritual birth and growth. We have an example in Hebrews 5, where immature Christians are likened to infants who need milk and not strong meat. If the spiritual life follows the same pattern as physical life, is it not possible that there is a spiritual gestation period between conception and birth? Is there not a time when new Christians are more like embryos, growing little by little in the womb, fed by the faith and vitality of others, just as a fetus lives by its mother's blood and sustenance?

Certainly we have all observed people who seemingly started well in the Christian life, blossomed and grew rapidly as new Christians, and yet, after a while, lost their spiritual vigor and faded away, sometimes into outright apostasy. This, of course, is just what the Lord predicted in the parable of the sower. "Some seed," he says, "fell on rocky places where it did not have much soil. It sprang up quickly . . . but when the sun came up, the plants were scorched and withered because they had no root." But the point is: *they did spring up!* There was life, but it could not bear the hot sun. As Jesus interpreted the parable: "The seed that fell on rocky places is the man who hears the word and at once receives it with joy, but since he has no root, he lasts only a short time. When trouble or persecution comes because of the word, he quickly falls away." Not having a root would correspond to the spiritual condition of not having any personal faith of his own. He lived for a while only on the faith (root) of others.

Again we must ask, What was the life that brought that initial experience of joy? Was it Spirit-given, or was it only a psychological response, coming from within the person alone? We probably cannot answer that question with any certainty. A similar case exists with the seed that fell among thorns and sprang up, only to be choked by the weeds which Jesus said were "the worries of this life and the deceitfulness of wealth." These two examples raise the possibility that there is Spirit-given life which is real and viable, but depends on proper care to come to fruit-bearing potential. It is only when it bears fruit that it can be called genuine grain, and it may be lost before it reaches that stage. Certainly Jesus said of the seed fallen in good soil that "it produces a crop." Viewing the parable in this light would make it almost a parallel to the situation in Hebrews 6.

But let us return to the metaphor of birth. Do we confuse conception with birth? A fetus may grow in the womb, fed by its mother's strength, but is that equivalent to birth? Of course not! Birth involves a break with the mother's life and the beginning of an independent existence that is peculiarly the infant's own. A newborn human may die after birth, even as everyone certainly will die in the normal course of events. But here the parallel with the spiritual must be altered, for many promises of Scripture powerfully assert that once born into the Father's family there is no way to lose that life! "I give unto them eternal life" says Jesus, "and they shall never perish!"

There is at least a hint of a prebirth spiritual gestation period in the promise of John 1:12: "Yet to all who received him, to those who believed in his name, *he gave the right to become children of God*—children . . . born of God." Here a "becoming" process is mentioned. This may be what Paul means when he writes to the Galatians, "My dear children, for whom I am again in the pains of childbirth until Christ is formed in you" (Gal 4:19). The critical question then becomes, When does an individual's faith become truly his own? Is he or she living off the faith of others, drawing true spiritual grace and life from them? This often seems the case with children raised in a Christian family. Their faith, which seems real enough as they are growing, is not yet their own. Only when they leave the family circle and are faced with the necessity of surviving in a hostile world do they either come to personal faith themselves or, sadly, abandon all pretense of faith and lose themselves in the world's unbelief.

The situation seems to be that borrowed faith, though real enough at the time to produce many signs of spiritual vitality, can be lost. Others, observing this, draw the conclusion that eternal life, once held, can be lost again. Theologians call that *Arminianism*, after a Dutch theologian named Arminius who held this view. Certain Scriptures seem to support it. But once faith truly becomes personal, it can never be lost, though it may waver and grow very weak at times. That is the conclusion of Calvinists. But who can really tell the difference? Only the Lord can! We must leave the matter then at that point, as Paul does in his letter to Timothy: "God's solid foundation stands firm, sealed with this inscription: 'The Lord knows those who are his,' and 'Everyone who confesses the name of the Lord must turn away from wickedness' " (2 Tim 2:19). God reads the hearts and knows whether the faith being exhibited is borrowed faith or genuine; it is only when that inward faith affects the outward life and the believer "turns away from wickedness" that we can tell it is genuine faith.

Bibliography

Barclay, William

    1957   *The Letter to the Hebrews.* Philadelphia: The Westminster Press.

Brown, Raymond

    1982   *The Message of Hebrews.* Downers Grove, Illinois: InterVarsity Press.

Bruce, F. F.

    1964   *The Epistle to the Hebrews.* The New International Commentary on the New Testament. Grand Rapids, Michigan: Eerdmans.

    1988   *The Canon of Scripture.* Downers Grove, Illinois: InterVarsity Press.

Buchanan, George W.

    1972   *To The Hebrews.* The Anchor Bible, Vol. 36. New York: Doubleday.

Calvin, John

    1949   *Commentary on the Epistle to the Hebrews.* Grand Rapids: Eerdmans.

Crabb, Larry
   1989   "Dealing with Sexual Sin," *Tabletalk* magazine.

Erdman, Charles R.
   1934   *The Epistle to the Hebrews.* Philadelphia: The Westminster Press.

Grant, F. W.
   1903   *Hebrews to Revelation.* The Numerical Bible. New York: Loizeaux Brothers.

Griffith-Thomas,
  W. H.
   1923   *Let Us Go On.* Chicago: The Bible Institute Colportage Association.

Guthrie, Donald
   1983   *Hebrews.* Tyndale New Testament Commentaries. Grand Rapids: Eerdmans.

Harrison, Everett F.
   1964   *Introduction to the New Testament.* Grand Rapids: Eerdmans.
   1971   *The Epistle to the Hebrews.*

Hawthorne,
  Gerald F.
   1969   *The Letter to the Hebrews.* A New Testament Commentary. Ed. G. C. D. Howley. Grand Rapids: Zondervan Publishing House.

Helyer, Larry R.
   1976   "The *Prototokos* Title in Hebrews." *Studia Biblica et Theologica.* Vol. 6, no. 2.

Henrichsen,
  Walter A.
   1979   *After The Sacrifice.* Grand Rapids: Zondervan.

Henry, Carl F. H.
   1986   *Christian Countermoves in a Decadent Culture.* Portland, Ore.: Multnomah.
   1989   "Shall We Fear God?" *Carl Henry at His Best.* Portland, Ore.: Multnomah.

Heschel, Abraham J.
  1975   *The Sabbath: Its Meaning for Modern Man.* New York: Farrar, Straus and Giroux.

Hewitt, Thomas
  1960   *The Epistle to the Hebrews.* The Tyndale New Testament Commentaries. Grand Rapids: Eerdmans.

Hughes, Philip
  Edgecumbe
  1977   *A Commentary on the Epistle to the Hebrews.* Grand Rapids: Eerdmans.

Howley, G. C. D.,
  Editor.
  1969   *A New Testament Commentary.* Grand Rapids, Michigan: Zondervan.

Kistemaker,
  Simon J.
  1984   *Exposition of the Epistle to the Hebrews.* New Testament Commentary. Grand Rapids: Baker Book House.

Lewis, C. S.
  1978   *The Problem of Pain.* New York: Macmillan.

MacArthur, John F.
  1983   *Hebrews: An Expository Commentary.* Chicago: Moody Press.

Mickelsen,
  A. Berkeley
  1960   *Hebrews.* The Biblical Expositor, Volume 3. Ed. by Carl F. H. Henry. Philadelphia: A. J. Holman Company.

Morris, Leon
  1983   *Hebrews.* Bible Study Commentary. Lamplighter Books. Grand Rapids: Zondervan.

Nouwen,
  Henri J. M.
  1989   *In the Name of Jesus: Reflections on Christian Leadership.* New York: Crossroad.

Owen, John
  1953   *Hebrews: The Epistle of Warning.* Abridgment by M. J. Tyron of 8 volumes. Grand Rapids: Kregel Publications.

Packer, J. I.
1986   *Your Father Loves You.* Ed. and compiled by Jean Watson. Wheaton, Ill.: Harold Shaw.

Peterson,
    Eugene H.
1987   *Working the Angles.* Grand Rapids, Mich.: Eerdmans.

Pettingill, William L.
1939   *Into the Holiest.* Wheaton, Illinois: Van Kampen Press.

Stedman, Ray C.
1974   *What More Can God Say?* Ventura, California: Regal Books.

Thiessen, Henry
    Clarence
1943   *Hebrews and the General Epistles.* Introduction to the New Testament. Grand Rapids: Eerdmans.

Wiley, H. Orton
1959   *The Epistle to the Hebrews.* Kansas City, Missouri: Beacon Hill Press.

Wescott, B. F.
1889   *The Epistle to the Hebrews.* London:Macmillan.

Wood, Nathan R.
1978   *The Trinity in the Universe.* Reprint. Grand Rapids, Mich.: Kregel.

Wright, Walter C.
1952   *Hebrews: A Guide for Bible Students.* Chicago: Moody Press.